ALABAMA BOY

An Architect's Memoir

By Frank Orr

Copyright © 2006 by Frank Orr

Alabama Boy
by Frank Orr
904 Huntington Circle
Nashville, TN 37215
615/319-2128

Printed in the United States of America

ISBN 1-60034-006-7

All rights reserved solely by the author. The author guarantees all contents are original and do not infringe upon the legal rights of any other person or work. No part of this book may be reproduced in any form without the permission of the author. The views expressed in this book are not necessarily those of the publisher.

Unless otherwise indicated, Bible quotations are taken from The Living Bible. Copyright © 1973 by Tyndale House Publishers, Inc., Wheaton, IL.

www.xulonpress.com

CONTENTS

FOREWARD ix
PROLOGUE xi
INTRODUCTION xv

PART ONE
    1. THE START 19
    2. FLORENCE 25
    3. SPIRITUAL LIFE 39
    4. MUSIC 47
    5. ATHENS 55
    6. FOOD 69
    7. BREAKING AWAY 75
    8. CARS 87
    9. UNCLE SAM 97
    10. NANCY 105
    11. FINDING FOCUS 117

PART TWO
    12. ARCHITECTURE 127
    13. A TRANSITION 149
    14. STEPPING OUT 153
    15. ORR/HOUK 165
    16. TRAVEL 203
    17. THE LAST WORD 215

APPENDIX I
Selected Works 225

APPENDIX II
Frank's A-List of Important Architectural Sites 235

INDEX 241

DEDICATION

To Nancy

FOREWORD

In 1998, Lake Providence Missionary Baptist Church formed a building committee to explore the possibilities of the relocation of our facility and congregation to the thirty-seven acre site we now occupy. This process required dedication and the collaboration of putting together the right team for the job.

As Pastor of the church, I knew that the most key ingredient for a successful project would be to find the right architect that felt the passion for our church ministry, and be able to put their dreams on paper and watch them develop into reality.

The process began with the interview of several architectural firms that were well known in the Nashville community. Many of those firms had very impressive portfolios of commercial buildings as well as churches. A recent project that our committee visited and inquired about held the key to begin our team. Our meeting with Frank Orr was not only a key element for a successful building project, but also a friendship that will last a lifetime. Frank's book, "Alabama Boy," tells of the life of a talented architect who was called into his profession as a minister is called to preach the gospel. Frank is a man who has an attention for detail that many would take for granted. The flow of a building is important for worship as well as its appearance. Frank is able to capture those details by interviewing the Pastor and ministry leaders. I thank God for this man, and it is my most fervent prayer that Frank will impart as much knowledge to those who follow in his footsteps.

God bless you, Frank!
Rev. Bruce Maxwell, Pastor
Lake Providence Missionary Baptist Church

April, 2005

PROLOGUE

It was October, 1957. Nancy and I had been married only about seven months, when we were shipped back to the States from Tripoli, Libya, where I had been stationed in the Air Force since 1955, leaving behind our first home, our honeymoon cottage. Our transportation was an ugly Army Transportation Command whopping big troop ship, named the USS Patch, that made a loop of Mediterranean ports to pick up and drop off military personnel, supplies, and such. We made several stops, including Athens, Rome (as a side trip) and Casablanca, a wonderful experience, but the most deeply affecting event, at least for me, was our stop at Istanbul.

Our arrival in Istanbul was anything but auspicious. There was some sort of political campaign going on, with parades, street protestors, a lot of noise, banners and maybe some gunfire. We were told to stay away from this. However, we were in a group of fellow travelers from our ship, and were safely sheparded around this kind of turmoil.

Before we left the ship, we signed up for a tour of the typical tourist sights – the Blue Mosque, the Topkapi Museum, etc. — all of which are memorable and worthy. After the tour we had lunch at the Istanbul Hilton. For us, two wet-behind-the-ears kids From Alabama, it was "high cotton." However, the highlight was the monumental Church/Mosque/Museum, Hagia Sofia.

From the outside the Hagia Sofia is rather dour and grungy looking. It is huge, a great mountain of a building, and it looms ever more sobering the closer you come. Once inside, though, this magnificent interior just overwhelms you, or at least that is what it did to me, and it justifies its reputation as one of the great architectural monuments of all time. I had heard of it, and read about it and seen pictures of it, but nothing had prepared me for the first hand experience of *being* there. The inventiveness of its design, utilizing new and untried structural concepts for its time, is no short of amazing. The grand space, corresponding to the nave in later churches, I suppose, astounded us by the sheer exuberance of the mosaics and other details, and even more so by the unexpected breadth of the spans of 250 feet by 100 feet, and the 175 foot interior clear height, unprecedented when it was completed in the year 532 AD. This, coupled with the interlocking half and full domes, which create the nature and character of the room, made it possible to construct in masonry, one of the world's most fulfilling spaces. Later, back in college, I made this drawing as an assignment in an architectural history class.

Figure 1: Hagia Sofia, Istanbul, Cutaway.

Its original design concept is so strong that the later conversions to a mosque and then to a museum could not diminish nor damage its sublime qualities of scale, space, and grandeur.

As a *complete* space, in my opinion it holds together better than St. Peters or St. Pauls, both of which are longer but narrower, and are much more ornate, and it was built over one thousand years earlier than either of these. One way to put it is to say that it is at "home with itself" in ways few other buildings have been able to achieve. Though immense, its designers and builders had found that exact "rightness," that fitness of scale we as architects always strive for. It is perhaps the most satisfying large space I have ever experienced.

I had had thoughts and maybe even dreams of becoming an architect before this experience in October 1957, but seeing the Hagia Sofia had the effect of crystallizing that vague ambition into a firm goal. As time went on I continued to seek to become an architect, and Nancy was right there with me, encouraging and literally at times supporting me, even when the goal seemed to be slipping away and circumstances seemed to be telling us it was not reasonable, and that we should take another, perhaps easier career track. It was a long and difficult trek. After that event Hagia Sofia became a touchstone for me, the one building that I always thought of when trying to make the best building I could. Even though I didn't always see everything through a spiritual prism during this architectural pilgrimage, I never lost sight of what I believed the Lord wanted me to be, and He came through. It happened, and I hope that the chapters of this book will explain how.

INTRODUCTION

"... every man has a map in his heart of his own country and .... the heart will never allow you to forget this map."
      Alexander McCall Smith, in his book,
THE NO. 1 LADIES' DETECTIVE AGENCY

There are several reasons for writing this, some of which I doubt if I fully understand or even consciously recognize. Among those I am aware of is a desire to acknowledge my Alabama roots, and how that heritage has shaped me. Although I have lived in other places, mainly in Tennessee, more years than in Alabama, being born and raised and indoctrinated in Alabama branded me in a way that even now still continues to find expression.

In no way is Alabama a perfect place, far from it. It has produced superior writers and musicians, and some rather creative politicians. It has had its blemishes rooted in the period when it was all right to use the "N" word, and unfortunately some of that is still around. It still suffers from a perception held in other parts of the nation as a place of bigotry and backwardness. True, perhaps, in some measure, but no worse than in other places in greater America. Among Southern states Alabama was in some ways a shade more progressive than her neighbors when I was growing up. It embraced more of the New Deal idealogy than some other nearby states, and apparently had a philosophy of being more open to the idea of government as the provider/protector, rather than the reluctant servant of the people.

Regardless, Alabama was my home in my most formative years. It shaped me and gave me most of my core values, both positively and negatively. Some things I observed or was taught in those early years I later found objectionable, and I rejected them. Some I have embraced. Whatever that history, Alabama just "is," and it is an inseparable part of me.

A second, though not subordinate, reason is to provide a record of that period, my growing up years, of the history of our time and place as I personally witnessed it, and perhaps I am the best person in our family to chronicle. We have always been a close family, with very few if any serious rifts, and we can usually find an open attitude and sympathetic ear with any member we may choose to contact. This was especially true for my brothers and me with our mother. And, I have found it frustrating and sad that she is no longer here to talk with. Mama died in 1997 at the age of 88, still alert in mind and active until physical health began to pull her down. Many times since I have thought of something about the family that I would like to know, and thought that I would ask Mama, and then sadly realizing that I could no longer do that. So, before it is too late for someone to ask, I want set to down what I remember or think I remember.

The structure of this book will be both topical and chronological, a mixture that may seem messy and arbitrary. I have inserted a number of special topical chapters in the chronological narrative, such as those titled Music, Food, and Cars. These I consider to be "Parallel" chronologies, and would not easily merge into the general flow of the story. I believe that the reader will understand this as the book is read. I apologize if this apparent anomaly offends anyone, but I find life itself messy and arbitrary, and I tend to think that life is not much fun unless you have a little messiness and uncertainty in it. That attitude toward "fun" may be an important part of what makes me what I am. This doesn't mean being frivolous; instead it means being "joyful." Maybe that will seep through in what I have to write. I recently told a friend that unless something is a matter of life or death I have a hard time keeping a straight face.

An example spontaneously bubbled up at a recent medical examination. I was being given an ultrasound test, similar to that given to expectant mothers, only this was for my heart. When the visual image first appeared on the monitor, I asked the technician, "Can you tell yet if it's a girl or a boy?" She didn't respond at all. A little later she turned on the sound, and it went something like "Whoosh-aah, Whoosh-aah." very reminiscent of the pinging sound of sonar. I thought but did not say, maybe because the tech didn't seem to appreciate my earlier witticism, "Have you located that submarine yet?"

When Nancy and I were in Morocco in 2002, traveling with a group of friends from earlier trips, I had occasional opportunities to offer spontaneous puns. While we were being bused around Rabat, we stopped for a walk around a market area, and were told to be careful of street vendors, some of whom would try to lure us into their establishments. Sure enough, were besieged by these people as we got off the bus, most of them shouting, "Come to my shop! Shake a leg! Shake a leg!" When we got off by ourselves I told the group that I had met the chief of this part of town, "Sheik Aleg."

As we approached Fez on this same trip, we saw a policemen directing traffic. I said, "Look, the fuzz of Fez!" Can you believe how bad that is?

My urge to engage in unsolicited humor has no doubt been a difficult thing for those around me, primarily Nancy, my wife, to bear. Those who know me are aware that I love a joke, especially if it is a pun, and the "groanier" the better. Maybe I'll sneak some of my favorites into this somewhere along the way.

This bent to humor bears a parallel to my attitude about architecture. I believe that life in general and architecture in particular should be joyful. One of the basics in architectural thought was first recorded by the Roman, Vitruvius, in the first century B. C. He said that architecture should be characterized by "Firmness, Commodity, and Delight." This might be modernized into, "Strength, Usefulness, and Joy." I not only believe that if a building is to be called architecture it has to have the quality of delight, but also that delight is frequently best expressed in a sense of humor, even in architecture. I further believe that any architect who doesn't have a good sense of humor should get out of the profession.

As for acknowledgements, dedications and the like, there are too many to list all who should be. I would, however, like to thank my parents, Frank Howard Orr, Jr., and Lola Ruth Lynch Orr, my brothers, Johnny and Allen, Nancy, my long-suffering wife, and my children and grandchildren, all for tolerating me and giving me such loving support even when it must have been very trying for them. In addition, my partner in architecture, Ed Houk deserves special thanks and praise, as do Bonna Whitten-Stovall for her editing, and Jim Sparks for his invaluable help.

*   *   *

I won't claim to have perfect memory; all I hope to do is to do the best I can, and have the discretion to play dumb and skip the specifics if I can't remember them. And if I feel I must depict anyone in an unflattering light I won't use their name, and will try to disguise them as much as possible. Any errors are my own. Amen.

PART ONE

1.

THE START

A man sent ten different puns to friends, in hope that at least one of the puns would make them laugh. Unfortunately, no pun in ten did.

I believe this has to be absolutely spellbinding to read, even to non-family members, but, what do I know?. Here is most of what I know about my antecedents.

I could start with a certain Charles Orr, our earliest known relative in this country, at least to me. He supposedly landed in Baltimore in 1725, from Ireland. There exists a body of information about the intervening folks between Charles and my grandparents, but I'll let others dig that out. On my mother's side similar documentation exists. I have copies of some of these records, which I'll pass on to my children, hoping they will know how to treat them. My mother's maiden name was Lynch, and some rather creative Lynch cousin crafted a construct in which we are descended from Charlemagne. The premise is that the name Lynch is a variation of Lintz, the town in Austria, supposedly founded by good old Charlemagne. And here I'd always thought that Lynch was pure Irish.

My Father's father was Franklin Howard Orr, born in 1866 in Morgan County, Alabama, with a twin brother, Will. Frank was a rather unsuccessful farmer. He married Penina (Nina) Amanda Ratliff around 1898, and began a family. For reasons unclear to me, he moved the family to a farm in or near Enterprise, Alabama when my father was young. Frank Howard, Jr., was born in 1907, the fourth child and third son in the family, and was called Howard. There were six children, three boys and three girls. Somehow the "lin" was dropped from his first name on his birth certificate. The rest of the clan must have seen something special in him because when he graduated from high school they all pooled their resources and sent him off to college. None of the others went past high school. He enrolled in the fall of 1925 in the School of Agriculture at Alabama Polytechnic Institute at Auburn, or API, (later changed to Auburn University), majoring in Poultry Science. He was living in a room attached to a chicken house during his second year when a fire wiped him out. He dropped out and went to Chicago and worked for a year with his eldest brother, Douglas, in construction, saving for his return to school.

While Daddy, or "Howard" was in college the family gave up the farm in Enterprise and moved to Birmingham. I don't believe my grandfather worked after that, dying of some form of cancer around 1935.

My grandmother, who we called "Orrie" (pronounced in our southern way, "Aw-ee"), was a family favorite, especially of all of her ten grandsons. There were no granddaughters until after she died.

I barely remember my grandfather, having only an image of him as a smiling, round-faced Irishman. Orrie I remember well. I have many fond memories of her little house, although it didn't seem little then, on Division Street in the Eastlake section of Birmingham. Even though during most of that time my family lived in Florence, Alabama, some 120 miles away, we would gather at Orrie's house several times a year. It was always a fun time for those of us in my generation. Those were some of the few times my brothers and I were able to spend time with our cousins. I was the oldest in our family, but my cousins, Buddy and Gene, sons of my uncle Louie, were older, and I looked up to them and enjoyed being with them.

They lived on a farm, and I envied them, and looked forward to visiting them there.

On my mother's side, I never knew her mother, but her father was around some of the time. By the time we all came along he was living in Mobile with my mother's half sister's family, but I only recall seeing him was when he visited us in Florence. My memory of him is of a tall, rather dour but dignified man. When I knew him he had a full head of iron gray hair and a big bushy mustache. His name was John Franklin Lynch, born in Lee County, Alabama in 1868, so I caught the name "Frank" from both sides of the family. My full name is Frank Howard Orr III. I vowed early in life that there would never be a fourth. John Lynch was a farmer and taught school some, continuing to live in Lee County until he was widowed for the second time and moved to Mobile. After losing his first wife, John married my mother's mother, Mary Belle Allen, from La Grange, Georgia. They had six children, three sons, followed by three daughters, adding to the four from his first marriage. My mother was the eldest of the second set of girls. She remained close to her sisters throughout their lives, and they were important influences on my life, and on my brothers' lives, as well. The middle sister was Elizabeth, or Libby. The youngest was Mary, who was only sixteen when I was born, and she spoiled me rotten all my life, even when she had children of her own. Libby was close, too. Her children were only slightly younger than we were in our family, so she didn't have the same opportunity to spoil me.

My parents married in 1930, and did not announce it right away. I have never been sure about the reason and the exact circumstances. It seems to have been an impulsive act, but the marriage survived, and grew increasingly stronger until my father's death in 1959. I came along in 1932. Then came Johnny Lynch in 1937 and Robert Allen in 1940. Being eight years old, and full of self-importance when Allen was born, I asked that he be named Robert, and be called "Bobby." We all called him Bobby for a few months, until Mama declared emphatically that his name was Allen, after her mother's family, and that is what he would be called.

Daddy worked for the Alabama Agricultural Extension Service his entire working life. He was still working when he died. He was working in Jasper, Alabama when I was born, and the family moved to the town of Florence in 1935. My memory of Jasper is limited, but I remember breaking my collarbone because I was standing up in the back seat of the car when Daddy made a sudden stop (what would the children's rights police make of that today?) Later, in Florence when I was about four, I broke my right leg when I was roughhousing and got it twisted under the sofa. And when I was in the seventh grade I broke that same collarbone showing off during lunch recess.

Once I strayed away from home in Jasper and some friends of my parents found me wandering along the street. They entertained me until the folks came for me. I vaguely remember sitting on what seems in my memory to be a baby grand piano, with a green cloth throw on top, dangling my feet over the edge. That is very likely a false memory, something in my imagination I dreamed up.

Our family was especially close to a family of church friends, named Standifer, who owned a restaurant, and had son, Bill, one year my junior. I loved going to the restaurant and climbing up on one of the stools at the soda fountain and spinning around. Jasper returned to my life at a much later age, and in a rather surprising way, a story we will hold till its time.

2.

FLORENCE

"Where is the Uffizi Palace, Mama?"

Both my brothers were born in Florence, Alabama. I went to school through the eighth grade there. My elementary school (we called it a "Grammar School" then) was Gilbert School, located in that part of town known as North Florence, near a complex intersection, known as "Seven Points." During my first grade we moved to a house on Beulah Avenue, right across the street from the side of the school. I could go home for lunch, and did often. One distinct memory of that time was a field trip to a cotton field, only a few blocks from the school. We walked there and were allowed to pick one boll each. Another memory is playing with my friends in the woods just a short block from our house.

In 1940, not long after I entered the third grade, and not long before my brother Allen was born in December, we moved into the first house my parents owned. It is at 714 Meridian Street, about two miles from Gilbert School. A few years ago Nancy and I went back to Florence, and I was devastated to find the school site now occupied by an apartment building. Thankfully, both houses were still there.

No school buses for us. I walked or rode my bike, or even sometimes skated. I didn't think anything of it, rather enjoying my walks home after because of what I could discover along the way. One day

I found an old broken guitar in an alley, and I took it home. I don't think I ever did anything with it, other than let it clutter up the house. Other untold treasures often got dragged home, too.

Those were carefree days in Florence, especially once we moved to Beulah Avenue. I had good friends living close by, Don Smith and Tommy Tewell. Jimmy Johnson lived just a few blocks away. We went to the same church as Jimmy's family. Another friend from school and church, George Chambers, lived in a different part of town. Jimmy, Tommy and I all liked to draw, and all of us eventually went into vocations using this aptitude. Tommy became a commercial artist, Jimmy, a sign painter, and I went into architecture.

This propensity for drawing perhaps came naturally and genetically for me. Mama had a strong artistic bent, producing several paintings early in her marriage. Sometime later, I suppose due to the demands of being a wife and mother she put it aside altogether. It was not until very late in her life that she took it up again, and she produced several pieces of serious worth. One thing I have marveled at is that so many times people I have known keep popping up in my life later on. Don was at Auburn part of the time I was in school there. I found out in the 1980's that Tommy had lived in Nashville for several years, but only discovered it when he joined our church. He died not too many years later. Jimmy also lives in Nashville and has for years. We recently renewed our friendship. George still lives in Florence; we have kept in touch sporadically over the years, but it was not until 2002 that we finally met again. It was a joyful reunion.

Family recreation was limited in those days, especially by today's standards. We went to movies as a family. Admission for adults was a quarter, and a dime for kids. Popcorn was a dime a bag. In those days that was all that was sold at the theater. On Saturdays the kids went without adults, for a double feature, one of which had to be a western — plus a cartoon, a serial, and two or three previews.

The other primary family activity was the Sunday afternoon drive. My folks would pile us into the car and drive around town and through the county. The rural part was a lot more attractive to Daddy because of his vocation. I never thought to ask what Mama thought about it, or if she would have preferred town. She never complained. Johnny and I did, though. Allen didn't come along until shortly before World War II and was too young to have much to say. By the time he was old enough to join in the War had started, and recreational driving was curtailed. Johnny and I would get bored in the back seat and get into arguments and drift into fights, sitting together in the back seat, facing what might be euphemistically called "corporal punishment" when we got home, that administered with a belt or a switch.

An architecturally significant event occurred around 1939, and I first became aware of it on those Sunday afternoon drives. The family that owned the local movie theaters in Florence and several neighboring towns was named Rosenbaum, and their adult and recently married son was building a new house. It was all the talk of the town. It looked unlike anything anyone had ever seen, and I was fascinated. His name didn't mean anything to me at the time, but it was designed by Frank Lloyd Wright, one of his Usonion designs. These projects were small houses that Wright developed a conceptual model for, affordable by people of modest means. They looked much like his larger houses for the rich and famous, but smaller. Maybe this was the beginning of my awareness of architecture as something magnetically drawing me to it.

The War

The years of World War II impressed me more than any other similar period of time. Tommy, Jimmy and I, and I am sure others our ages spent a lot of time and used up a lot of notebook paper drawing fighter planes, tanks, submarines and other war machines in combat situations.

When my granddaughter, Mary Katherine Moore, was eleven she called one evening asking if she could interview me for a school assignment. The central question, when she arrived was, what life was like in general and my life in particular was like when I was her age. The more we talked the more I remembered. Soon I realized that my eleventh year was in the middle of World War II, 1943-44. I told her that much of what life was like then was because of the war, and that it wouldn't have been that way if the country had not been at war. We had rationing of everything from gasoline to sugar to tires. When I went to Boy Scout camp the summers of 1943 and 1944 I had to take my own little jar of sugar if I wanted any. Everyone collected paper, tin cans and scrap metal. In the fourth grade I collected more paper than anyone else in our school. The next year they started handing out "Eisenhower Medals" for the most collections. I didn't win that year and was a little chagrinned because I didn't get a medal, but I soon got over it because the war effort was so much more important for me and everyone than any medal would be. Housewives saved cooking grease and turned it in to be used in making munitions. We had meatless Tuesdays. We had air raid drills at school. Because his job was considered essential, (and probably because of his age) Daddy did not serve in the military, although he had been in the National Guard at one time. His job was to look after the needs and welfare of farmers, making sure they had what they needed to keep the food supply for the nation going.

Among his duties was to enlist farmers to try out new agricultural ideas and technologies, proposed primarily by TVA, the Tennessee Valley Authority . One of those was the use of liquid ammonia for fertilizer. Maybe because he couldn't get anyone else to agree to it, he persuaded my uncle Louie to allow him to conduct the experiment on Louie's farm. Daddy found somewhere an old flat bed truck with no doors. On the bed he had mounted, secured with chains, a large cylindrical tank. A pipe had been tapped into the tank at the rear, to which was attached a cross pipe with several holes at regular spacing. The main pipe had a valve, and I was told to sit on the back of the truck bed, and turn the valve on when Daddy gave me a signal. Daddy drove as we headed out across the field, and Johnny was riding with him. Daddy started to drive across a terrace, a kind of earthen berm built along contour lines, to control water flow to the best advantage for crops. He attacked at too sharp an angle, and the truck began to lean, and toppled over. I jumped off of the rear and Johnny jumped out of the front, conking his head, but not injuring him seriously, at least as far as I can tell!

Then the fun began. The ammonia began to spill out and flood the field, in a much higher concentration than intended. The truck was laying on its side, and a helper, or just observer, I never knew which, decided to climb up the exposed bottom frame of the truck to see what might be done. As soon as he got to the now top side, the fumes hit him and he toppled over and off the truck, knocked totally out. He must have been revived, otherwise there would have been more stink in the press than in the field. I never found out the official outcome of this experiment. It probably was abandoned.

Mama worked for the county Welfare Department during that time. Her office was in an otherwise vacant store building in North Florence. They didn't need all the space in the building so the rear of the store was used as a collection place for the paper and such gathered for the war effort. I sometimes went there after school to look through those materials, just out of boyhood curiosity. Among other things collected were old phonograph records, presumably because of the shellac in them. I remember seeing a big, thick one-sided record by Enrico Caruso. I vaguely knew who Caruso was, but we didn't have a record player so I never listened to it. One of the things I picked up on my rounds collecting paper and metal was a World War I German helmet. The son of the lady who donated it had brought it back from that war. It was beautiful, covered in leather and in perfect condition. I wonder if it was turned in for scrap metal, or if someone kept it as a souvenir.

Florence is on the north bank of the Tennessee River as it swings across North Alabama. One time a flood notice was issued and Daddy had to go out, after dark, and warn farmers to move their livestock up out of bottom land. It was summertime and I went with him. On the way home after reaching all the farmers he could we had a blowout. We changed the tire to the spare, which was slick and showing cords. We crept very carefully back to town, even though we had to move fast because the river was steadily rising. We made it OK, but it was only because of the essential nature of his job that he was even able to buy a new tire. Everyone else had to wait or do without.

Daddy was also an air raid block warden. On designated nights we would have air raid drills, and every night everyone would have to make sure that their blackout window shades were in place, leaking no light. The air raid warden's job included checking on light-leaking windows and other sources of light. The purpose was to keep enemy aircraft from being able to navigate by following light from the ground.

It was a deadly serious time, and everyone, I mean everyone, was involved in the "War Effort." All young boys were encouraged to join the "Junior Commandos." We had drills of our own. At regular meetings we studied small hard black plastic models of enemy aircraft so we could recognize them. We also had flip cards with the plane silhouettes on one side and the names on the other. We were to sound an alert when we saw them overhead. We wore "cool" armbands, with a variation of the Civil Defense logo on them. We were fingerprinted. Air raid wardens wore pith helmets with the logo, plus armbands. Different functional units had different symbols in the middle, indicating their specialty, but the overall logo was the same, a white circle with a red triangle in the center, and the specific service symbol inside that.

We were also encouraged to contribute to the war effort by buying War Bonds, which we could do in small incremental steps by buying twenty-five cent savings stamps and pasting them in little books, very much like the old S & K stamp books that were all the rage in the mid 20th century. When you filled a book you had paid only $18.75 for the stamps, but it could be turned in for a $25.00 War Bond, which would mature in ten years. Bonds and stamps were sold many places, including the lobbies of movie houses. Movie stars participated in "Bond Drives," appearing at special shows to urge folks to "Buy Bonds." I seem to remember that one of the stars appearing in Florence was Ann Sheridan. There was often a notice with the film credits at the end urging everyone to "Buy Bonds," which they could do in the Lobby of "this very theater." Sometimes even now you can see this notice on an old film you see on television.

A miniature Japanese submarine our Navy had captured was hauled around the country on a flat bed truck, to show what this dreaded enemy was up to, and to inspire us all to greater war support, and buy more bonds.

We were all taught to be especially careful of what we said and where we said it, being cautioned, "Loose lips sink ships." A company making and selling yoyos had employed a yoyo star, supposedly a Filipino, to go around the country, demonstrating how to do all sorts of yoyo tricks, and of course, selling yoyos. Word got around that the star was a Japanese spy, and we were all told to avoid his shows. I'm sure now it was all bunk, but given the mood of the country, bunk I can understand.

When the war was finally over in 1945 virtually everyone had played a part, and we all believed a vital part, in reaching victory. Everyone past age five or so, enlisted wholeheartedly in the war effort, and were proud to do so. We rejoiced in victories and wept for those killed and injured, and for their families. Everyone knew someone who had gone away to fight, and everyone knew of one or more who would not be coming back. Jimmy Johnson had an older brother who had joined the military and had gone off to fight. Jimmy's father was the Director of the Junior Sunday School Department of our church. ("Junior" meant grammar school age). One Sunday morning, with tears in his eyes, he announced to the Department that Jimmy's brother had been killed. This kind of thing happened over and over, and it touched all of us deeply.

Windows in houses displayed small banner-type flags to show that a person from that home was in service, with silver stars if they were alive, gold if they had died. Those years of national sacrifice and unity impressed me so deeply that till this day I tend to think of that kind of national atmosphere as the norm, and what we have seen since as an aberration.

There have been other wars since then, some with a major nation-wide scale of involvement, such as Korea, Viet Nam and Iraq, but none has matched the nature and intensity of what we experienced during WWII, and in many ways we are the poorer for it.

Other Childhood Memories

While we still lived in Jasper my folks brought home a companion for me, a Boston terrier we named Rowdy. He was my true buddy.

He was brindle, with one blue eye and one brown. Even though he snored and sometimes smelled and had to be fed too often, and bathed, there couldn't have been a better friend for me. In those days kids were given a lot of freedom to roam without much supervision, and Rowdy and I went everywhere together. Rowdy was "bad" to chase cars, and even caught one occasionally, to his regret, for he acquired several scrapes and scars over the years. He lived to be about eleven, finally having been brought down by a city bus he caught but was unable to corral.

Christmases were important times for us. Sometimes we went to Birmingham and stayed at Orrie's house. During the war, with restrictions on gasoline, we usually stayed in Florence. Our Christmas stockings were real work socks, gray with red banding on the top, heel, and toe, about a foot and a half long. We could always expect to find some candy, fruit, nuts and small toys in them, and always an orange in the toe. One wartime Christmas our major gifts were recycled things our parents found and bought from friends whose children had outgrown them. I specifically remember Johnny got a football that was so worn that it had the texture of suede, but it was treasured just the same. It wasn't that our folks couldn't afford new toys; there just weren't many available. Another gift that year, to both Johnny and me, was a big metal bus, almost two feet long. It had been repainted, I'm sure by Daddy. Another year, there was a stuffed monkey doll for each of us boys, made out of the same kind of work socks used for our Christmas stockings, hand crafted by Orrie. We didn't care much for dolls, but we treasured those monkeys just the same, because they had been made for us by the only grandmother we ever knew.

A marvelous black lady named Amanda Simpson was our "Help" in Florence, but was so much more. Although we didn't use the term at that time, she was our Nanny, and because Mama worked most of her adult life, Amanda in a very real sense raised my brothers and me. She kept us in clean clothes, and fed us lunch when we weren't in school, and disciplined us just the same way our parents would have. That meant a good walloping when we needed it, which no doubt was often. She must have loved us; I never had any doubts about that. She couldn't have put up with our orneriness if she hadn't. I know that I loved her dearly. I told Mama one time that Amanda was my "other Grandmother," and I still think of her that way. This experience, no doubt, was not limited to me and my brothers, and has contributed to a closeness between the races among those of similar backgrounds. Even after our move to Athens we kept touch with her. Our last contact with her was when Nancy and I were married, we sent her an invitation, and she sent us a modest but very nice gift, a tablecloth, I think.

Our family went to First Baptist Church every time the doors were open. Daddy was a Deacon, and Sunday School Superintendent for a time, among various other positions of responsibility. Mama had been a Methodist all her life, but was fully Baptist actively if not officially. I was taken, sometimes to my great reluctance, along to all the activities I was supposed to attend. For the most part I enjoyed them. One special group was the Royal Ambassadors, or RA's, a mission study organization for boys in the same approximate age range as the Boy Scouts. I went to two summer RA camps, and at the second I felt a strong desire to become a missionary. Looking back, I can see that I was greatly influenced by a furloughing missionary from Japan, who spoke several times during that week. Of course it was during the war and Japan was the enemy, and the message was that Japan needed the Gospel. I don't remember his name, but the missionary was soft spoken and gentle in his demeanor, not forceful like many preachers I had heard. He seemed to be the kind of person I would like to be. At the last service there I made a public commitment to Jesus as my Savior, and to dedicate my life to be a missionary. I never became the kind of missionary I envisioned then, but the intense desire to be involved in loving and serving the people of the world has never left me. Later that year I went forward in a service at our church to acknowledge my acceptance of Jesus as my Savior, and for baptism and church membership. Mama went with me, finally becoming a Baptist officially, and a few days later we were both baptized at the same service. I was eleven.

Even though it was a time of war and sacrifice, those were days of joy and freedom for boys my age. When the weather got warm enough I took off my shoes and put them on only on Sunday until around October. Yes, children, I went to school barefoot. I sometimes wore bib overalls without a shirt, also to school. It wasn't that we couldn't afford clothes; it was just that I didn't want to wear any more than modesty required during warm times.

As for what we now call race relations, I have to confess that I was not very aware of any overt conflict. Amanda was primarily the cause of that because of the very great influence she had on me. There were other black people around, and our contact always seemed to me to be cordial, if distant for the most part. Of course we didn't go to the same schools, but that and church were about the only places the two found formal and rigid separation.

Despite living in the culture we did, my parents always taught us to be tolerant, taught us to have respect for all people, not only the Negroes, which was the polite term in those days for African Americans, but also for Jews. There was a small number of them in Florence, but they were fairly visible. The Rosenbaum family, mentioned earlier, was perhaps the most prominent. Another group that Daddy had great respect for were the German immigrant families who had settled in a farming community north of Florence, named St. Florian, pronounced locally: "St. Floreen." They were hard working, friendly folks, totally Americanized, having been in this country many generations. I always enjoyed going to this German community with Daddy, and spending time with them. If there was animosity toward them during the War, I was not aware of it.

Nonetheless, reflecting on the experiences my generation had growing up in a small town in the South, and observing both races for seventy-plus years, it seems to me that at least among those who grew up in the South in that period there is more similarity than difference between the races. One incident from my childhood comes to mind every so often. My buddies and I liked to play football every chance we got. This was the school boy equivalent of "Smash Mouth" football of that day. We played tackle without pads or helmets or any other protection. It's a wonder no one was ever seriously injured. About all anyone suffered was bruised pride. Scratches and dings were signs of manliness. We played in someone's backyard, or on the school playground after school, or on the lawn of a very nice city park in the middle of town. One favorite playing field was the church side yard, where we played after attending RA meetings. This was usually on Saturday.

One Saturday a black boy about our age showed up, not for the meeting, though he probably would have been welcome if it were left up to us boys. We invited him in to the game and he turned out to be as good or better than anyone else. He came back a couple of other times. There should have been more experiences like this. We would all have benefited if there had been. I am truly sorry for all the pain and inequities suffered by blacks in America in general and Alabama in particular. I would like to say that I have grown up to be completely unprejudiced, but you probably know that is impossible. I am still a work in progress.

After graduating from Gilbert School I went to Florence Junior High School for the seventh and eighth grades. It was only three blocks from our house on Meridian Street, so I continued to walk or bike to school. For the first time I had to go to different classrooms, and have different teachers for different subjects. I had always gotten along fairly well with my grammar school teachers, but some of these in Junior High were a little hard to take. I had always been an indifferent student, aware that I could do better. In today's jargon, I just wasn't motivated enough. I drifted along, enjoying life, promising myself that I would do better at some future time.

Located in the northwest corner of Alabama, Florence was for me, and I suppose still is for most others who have lived there, a very special place. Founded by Andrew Jackson, as he and his company established the Natchez Trace between Nashville and Natchez. In 1818 Jackson, then President James Madison and several others invested in a new development company, named "The Cypress Land Company." The town itself was named by Fernand Sannoner, the engineer who laid out the new town. He declared that the terrain reminded him of his hometown, the Italian Florence. Nice story, but when I finally got to visit the Italian version in 1995 I didn't see much similarity, although both are situated on the banks of impressive rivers. The Alabama Florence has its own kind of character and charm. Florence is not much like the typical southern county seat town in appearance. The most prominent physical feature is not the traditional courthouse square, but a long straight grand boulevard beginning from a high point on the north, anchored by an imposing mansion, and sweeping down from there to the river bank perhaps two miles away. A grid of streets extends east and west from this central spine. The result is a town of grace and beauty, a great place for a young boy to grow up in, particularly if he has imagination, and what young boy doesn't?

As the terrain extends toward the north, away from the river, the terrain of Florence begins to become rather hilly. Our home territory around Meridian Street was no exception. Johnny and I were known to get in our Radio Flyer coaster wagon and fly down the street three or four blocks from the house. At the bottom of the hill we would merge into another, wider and more heavily trafficked street, dodging cars, trucks and the occasional horse-drawn wagon, and causing great consternation to all but the two of us. For us it was a great thrill.

Meridian Street terminates on the north just one house lot from ours. This intersecting street goes downhill at an ever more accelerating rate, ending in a "T" intersection three blocks down. Opposite the end was a billboard. One day two of my friends were "doubling" on a bicycle, a common local practice, racing down this hill, and somewhere along the way decided to change positions enroute. All went well until the fellow moving to the front was lowering himself onto the bar, and unintentionally, of course, stuck his foot through the spokes of the front wheel. They and the bike jumped the curb and went tumbling forward, chewing up grass and dirt, ending up flying through the air and slamming into the billboard, doing considerable damage to the bike and themselves. Both survived, though, with relatively minor injuries.

Sometimes some of us would just go out on our bikes and see what we could see. We might pedal over the river bridge at Florence, through the town of Sheffield on the south bank, turn east and cross back across the river over Wilson Dam, and then home. It was a ride of probably twenty miles. A bicycle was indispensable for boys, and many girls as well, in that time. Many services were delivered to homes and neighborhoods by horse, or mule-drawn wagons. Produce was sold on the streets in front of our houses from wagons driven into town from nearby farms. Another common sight were wagons from the ice house, delivering ice to homes that didn't have refrigerators, and there were many of them. We boys liked to pull up on our bikes behind an ice wagon, grab hold of it, and let it pull us along for a while.

In the spring of 1946, Daddy got a new job, still with the Extension Service. Where he had been an Assistant County Agent in Jasper and Florence, he now had responsibility for certain more narrowly focused programs in some fifteen counties in North Alabama. This required us to move to Athens, about 45 miles east, but we would wait until school was out.

At thirteen I was distressed and torn at the thought of leaving my Florence friends, and giving up my expectation of eventually graduating with them from Coffee High School. Because things pass quickly for teenagers, I suppose, I soon came to be at peace with it all. During that first summer our family rented rooms on the second floor of a large, older house near the middle of town, while a new house was being built for us. At the time, our new house was on the far western edge of town, but only about a mile from the Courthouse Square. As time passed over the years the town grew and now this place is closer to the center than to the edge. Because it was so soon after the end of the war, supplies and building materials were scarce, and some adjustments and sacrifices to quality had to be made. Nonetheless, it was our home until we each left for college, and it was our parent's home for the rest of their lives.

3.

SPIRITUAL LIFE

There was a shipwreck and the only two survivors washed up onto a deserted island. After a brief conversation they discovered that they both were Baptists. They immediately had a prayer, sang a song, took up a collection and set a goal for three for the next Sunday.

The place of church, in particular, and spiritual life, in general, has always been a constant and essential part of my life. When I joined the church in 1943 I had been immersed in the life of the church since before I was conscious of it. I have already shared the details of this in the previous chapter.

I have a problem with formalized plans of sharing the gospel with the unsaved, those that tell us to start by telling what our life was like before accepting Jesus, and what had changed afterward. Because I had always known about Jesus and knew that He was my Savior, joining the church just made it public. So, I've never been a good evangelizer. I have been through formal witnessing training programs, like Evangelism Explosion and a similar one Baptists copied from it, and they didn't "take" with me. They are just too rigid, and suffer from a malady I have observed in other areas of human activity that I see as a "one size fits all" philosophy. One size rarely fits all, and the attempt to make it so just boxes us in, and limits us to only the one way we have been taught. When a new challenge comes along, something outside the bounds of the "program," we have no tools with which to respond to it. We are left dangling, and the result likely will be that we will be embarrassed and the purpose of our efforts damaged.

However, I continued to be as active in church life as anyone could wish all through my growing up years, and I generally was happy doing so. I went, or in some cases was dragged, to every offering of the church had for my age group. This included not only Sunday school, but also the Sunday evening groups, called Baptist Training Union, or BTU. There were BTU camps in the summertime, usually held at the Alabama Baptist state assembly grounds, called Shocco Springs. I believe I went to two as a teen. At one of these I met a bright, attractive young lady, and corresponded with her some afterward. Nothing came of that, but maybe it shows that I had more earthly interests as well.

When I went off to college, I drifted into letting those other interests become more dominant my life than they should have been. Of course, academic things had to take up a lot of time and energy, but social life was not neglected. At that time Auburn was on the quarter system. The beginning of the winter quarter of my freshman year I pledged a fraternity, and soon it was becoming even more important than either school or church. Even though the fraternity was a major distraction I have mixed feelings about it. I have a few fast friends from those days that even today I could call on for help if needed.

In 1954 I left Auburn without graduating and joined the Air Force. During my almost four years in the USAF, I hope through a maturing process, many changes came. I got married, got serious about finishing my degree, and most important, began to get more serious about my spiritual life. I had never totally abandoned it, just didn't pay much attention to it for a time. It wasn't until Nancy and I married and the seriousness of that life status began to sink in that I started to try to return to my spiritual roots.

When I was discharged from the USAF in the spring of 1958 Mark, our first child was on the way, and I had to go to work. We lived in our hometown of Athens, Alabama, and I found a job in Huntsville, twenty-six miles to the east. Just two weeks after our second son, Steve, was born, I started back to college at Auburn, in the fall of 1959. By that time Nancy, who had been raised a Methodist like her mother-in-law, had joined our Baptist church in Athens. In Auburn, there was a small church where a lot of married students and their families attended. We joined there and were soon heavily involved. After finally graduating I found a job in Nashville, and we joined Woodmont Baptist Church in the spring of 1962.

Settling into my roles as a husband, father, and primary wage earner, I soon found that church was going to be as important a part of my life as it had been to my parents. I began to be involved in a number of activities and ministries, serving on committees, and teaching Sunday School among others. In Sunday School I taught nine year old boys and twelve year old boys one year each, and a coed college class for several years. In 1968 I was elected Deacon and served continually, three years out of every four, for the rest if the time the family stayed at Woodmont.

Among Baptist churches the roles of Deacons vary, but the most common pattern, and the one found at Woodmont, is that these members, almost always men but occasionally women, are elected to assist the Pastor in his ministerial duties, *not* to serve as a Board of Directors.

Obviously, music is a crucial part of worship in almost any church. It had been for me all through my growing up years. In high school I had sung in the adult church choir. One stretch of that period my brother Allen was the music director. When we had settled in Nashville and at Woodmont, and the kids had become teens and migrated to their contemporaries' groups and activities, I decided to join the church choir. Woodmont had a very strong music ministry. Being located in Music City USA meant they we had some real music pros in the Church. At the second rehearsal I attended, the piece being worked on was The Messiah. I found myself seated between two of the most musically adept and strongest voices in the whole church – Bob Mulloy, head of the Music Business Department at Belmont College, and Ken Holland, who with his very talented wife, Lois, for many years provided musical support for evangelical ministries all over the country. It was just a coincidence that they were not on the road at that time. I was literally blown away. I couldn't hear myself think, much less sing. I never went back after that, contented to be one who sits in a pew, content to try to "make a joyful noise."

An important sea shift occurred at Woodmont in 1977. Earlier the Church had established a house for furloughing missionaries. The residents at that time were Clark and Sara Scanlon, from Guatemala. Shortly before the Scanlons arrived in 1976 there had been a massive earthquake in Guatemala, killing some 17,000 people and destroying whole cities. Clark, who had been intensely involved in the recovery work there, was inspired to organize a team from Woodmont to go to Guatemala to help rebuild a damaged church building. That was the first any of us had heard of volunteer missions, though this has now become a major movement among evangelical Christian groups. My business partner, Ed Houk, and I both volunteered to go, agreeing that only one of us could be out of the office at the same time. Ed was chosen and I stayed home for that two-week period. Instead, a little later I went with a different group to a Chicago suburb to help with a renovation project at a small church there. Clark documented the entire Guatemala episode in a book, Hope In The Ruins, (Broadman Books, 1978).

The next year Clark asked me to go to Guatemala City alone for an architectural consultation to the Baptist mission there for a couple of projects. There were four or five missionary couples plus a single girl in the city at the time, and several couples living out in the countryside away from Guatemala City. My two tasks were to consult on the design of a new missionary residence for the Scanlons and whoever might need it later, and a master plan of a large complex of ancient buildings the mission owned in the middle of town, then used as a bookstore, mission offices, and for various other things.

That trip was a monumental eye-opening experience. I was hooked! I could see for the first time the vital work missionaries did, and the difficulties and hardships they had to endure, which they did gladly. I identified with them, and wanted to help them in any way I could. In addition, I could meet local people and could begin to understand how they responded to the Gospel, and to understand how the missionaries tried to minister to them. In the master planning project a Guatemalan was assigned to help me measure and take down other data. Neither of us spoke enough of the other's language, but, through sign and body language, and a few words and gestures we were able to communicate all we needed to. As in other places I went to on mission trips later, it was a joy to just be with people who were on fire for the Lord, and weren't reticent in showing it.

After this initial experience I began to look for opportunities to go on mission trips. The volunteer missions movement was becoming nation-wide in scope, not only in Southern Baptist churches, but also among many other denominations and individual churches. I had found my special place of service. In 1980 Nancy and I went with a group to Aytec, Mexico, and with another team to Guatemala again in 1982, both renovation and construction projects. I was put in charge of the 1982 trip, a team of eighteen of all ages. Our project was to do extensive renovations to the buildings of a theological seminary, located in Guatemala City, away from the center of town. Also, with Chris Magill, another architect on the team, I went to prepare a master plan for a satellite campus of the seminary, located on beautiful Lake Atitlan, in the mountains, west of Guatemala City. Guatemala is an entrancing country. The missionaries called it "The Land of Perpetual Spring," and it certainly seemed so the two times I was there. Year round it would rain a little in the early afternoon, and have absolutely gorgeous weather all the rest of the time, year round.

In 1985 our furloughing missionaries staying in the Woodmont missionary house were Bert and Ruth Dyson, who had originally gone out from Woodmont to the mission field to Nigeria. They had completed thirty years of service there, and, when most people would be thinking about retiring, had agreed to start a new missions work in the West African country of Sierra Leone. Bert proposed to the church that Woodmont establish a more or less permanent relationship with the Sierra Leone Baptists and send construction teams there on a continuing basis. I was asked to lead that program, and I organized most of the six or seven teams that went there.

The initial project was to help build one of several residence buildings at a conference center located on the campus of a hospital at the town of Lunsar. This facility had been started and supported by European Baptists some years earlier, and Southern Baptists from America were then helping there with financial support and some medical staff. Each of our two teams of seven in that first trip stayed two and a half weeks, overlapping the middle week. I was in the first group. One special blessing of this trip was that there were three Auburn architects on the team; both of the others, Kenny Beam and Garry Askew, are a good deal younger than I.

On the return trip from Sierra Leone we had a bit of adventure. Our team of six men and one woman was delayed leaving Freetown because of a mechanical problem with the hydraulic system serving the landing gear of the airplane. For some reason it was decided to go ahead and depart, and two or so hours after our scheduled departure time we took off and flew on to Monroeville, Liberia, the next scheduled stop for this KLM flight. It was to have flown on to Casablanca and then to Amsterdam, where we would have caught a trans-Atlantic flight to Atlanta, and home. There a major change of plans developed. The KLM folks must have thought they could get the necessary repairs done in Monroeville, but they discovered that a new part was needed, and by the time it had been flown in from Amsterdam it would be too late for the plane to leave that night. We all had to spend an unplanned night in Liberia.

We walked to a rather nice hotel across the road from the airport, where KLM put us up and fed us both dinner and breakfast. Next morning, however, there was no sign of the needed part and no prospect of any KLM flight that day.

The KLM personnel scurried around, I suppose, trying to find us all alternate flights, all meaning the entire passenger complement of the flight, which would be going to many different destinations. We all sat around the airport waiting for some word of a flight, any flight, home.

Being in charge of our team, I was responsible for everyone, at times quite a challenge. Shortly before we arrived there had been an attempted coup in Liberia, and the airport was locked down and crawling with fierce looking men in uniforms, carrying machine guns. We were told that morning to absolutely not take any photos. One member of our team failed to take this in and blithely went around with his little Instamatic camera shooting pictures. I didn't know this until I was tapped on the shoulder, and turning, met a soldier with my friend in tow. In almost incomprehensible English I was commanded to accompany the two of them to the office of the airport Security Chief for what we feared could be detention of some unknown duration, or perhaps, worse. Arriving at the office door, we found it locked. We waited several minutes until, finally, the soldier took away the offending camera and told us we could go. Afterward, my friend told someone in the group that he had lost the lens out of the camera, and that the pictures would probably not have been any good anyhow.

We finally were put on a British Airways flight, and went to London, where we had another unscheduled overnight, at KLM's expense, and then on a flight to Atlanta and home the next day.

Two years later another team had been organized, with me, again as leader. We were to depart New Years Eve, but on Christmas Eve I was hit by a mild heart attack. From the hospital I arranged for my 1985 roommate, Kenny Beam, to take over as leader. He did an excellent job; maybe better than I would have. This team built a small church building in Makene, a short distance from Lunsar. Our firm produced the construction drawings for it. In 1988 Bert asked me to go back to Sierra Leone for architectural consultation, which I did, and tried to help in several places for a number of projects.

Over the years our architectural firm also provided construction documents for church projects in Panama, Honduras, Mexico, Poland, Benin, and Canada.

Since then Nancy and I have been to Poland for an architectural consultation, and to Portugal with a team of close friends to try to teach English as a second language to Portuguese folks. As in all mission trips, we had several training sessions at the Church, having folks who were experienced in doing what we were planning to do, help us to be prepared.

I went to Brazil in 2000 on a construction project. Our team of fifteen, working with a dozen or so talented and hard working Brazilians, we were able to build, in a small town not far from Rio, a complete church building from the slab up, in five-and-a-half days. This included walls, roof, wiring, painting and all other finishes, and even building the pulpit and pews. I continue to look for opportunities like these, and expect to find them, and to respond as long as I am able.

Concurrently with this pro bono activity, my architectural practice moved ever more toward a specialization in church design. I was and am convinced that this has been my calling, as surely as, and in the same way that a Pastor has a calling. I have had full support in this from my partner, Ed Houk, who has been not only the strong managing hand needed for our firm, but also a steadfast friend and spiritual guide.

I suppose my basic Christian testimony is this:

As I have recounted, early in my life I was convinced that the Lord wanted me to be a missionary. There came a time when I was equally convinced that I was supposed to be an architect. This tension came to a crisis point when I had been discharged from the Air Force and had to decide on a career and the education it required. Not only was it important for me individually, but obviously it would affect my family as well. I prayed about it, and talked with my Pastor and others, and just waited on the Lord to let me know. As time went by indicators for missions began to wane and those for architecture began to open up. Eventually I felt no confusion; I went back to Auburn to finish college in architecture. Since graduation I have continued to work in architecture, most of the time as a Principal. At the same time the Lord put opportunities in my path to participate in volunteer missions and other avenues of service. I have decided that He intended me to be *both* an architect and a missionary, but on *His* timetable, not mine.

4.

MUSIC

If it ain't Baroque, Don't Fix It

*A*side from church music, which I mentioned in the previous chapter, music wasn't always that important for me. Growing up we didn't have a piano until my Aunt Libby Vandiver and her children came to live with us during World War II. Her husband, "Vandy," had been called into the Army. I don't remember how long they stayed with us, but they brought with them a lot of furniture, including a big console radio that sat on the floor and had a built-in record player, and a huge, very ornate upright piano. We had a radio, of course. Everybody we knew did. Ours was one of those round-top Philcos. I wish I had it now.

We listened to WSM in Nashville, mostly for farm market reports, weather reports, and such. However, WSM had a show on Sunday afternoons called "Sunday Down South" on which they played live music by their studio band. They also had symphonic music, which I didn't pay much attention to at the time, and, of course, The Grand Ole Opry. We called country music "Hillbilly" then, and I didn't much care for it, although I since have come to appreciate it and even enjoy much of it, especially Blue Grass.

There were other stations that we listened to, I suppose, but WSM is the only one I can remember by name. I liked to listen to the adventure serials, Terry and the Pirates, The Shadow, and some others, and the whole family listened to evening comedy shows like Jack Benny, Fred Allen, and Fibber Magee and Mollie. Personally I listened to nighttime adventure shows like Your FBI in Peace and War, and Mr. District Attorney, all of which is getting away from "music."

While we had the piano Mama signed me up to take piano lessons. They didn't take. I lasted about seven months and sweated through one recital before Mama and the teacher, who lived across the street, decided that my talents, if any, lay elsewhere.

Many years later, when our kids were approaching the age where piano lessons would be the thing to do, I called Libby and asked her whatever happened to that piano. She said that she had lent it to their church, but if I wanted it, I could have it. The only difficulty was that I would have to come get it. The Vandivers lived in Cullman, Alabama, about 150 miles south of Nashville, so I arranged to rent a trailer, and I cajoled Earl DuRard, one of my employees, to go with me to pick it up. When we got there, Libby met us at the church and we went inside to get the piano. We looked all over, class rooms, the Fellowship Hall, anywhere it might have been, but it was nowhere to be found.

Finally one of the church staff told us he thought it had been sold. After a little negotiating, the Church agreed that Libby could take one of equal age and type to replace it. We found one and Earl, who was a musician of sorts, tried it out and pronounced it fit for its purpose. Then we loaded it up and drove back to Nashville. It did not have near the exuberant, Victorian visual character of the original, but as far as I could determine the musical quality was much the same. When it had served its purpose and all of our kids had a go at piano lessons, we donated this piano to a Nashville Korean church. Many years later my firm was asked to donate design services to this church for an addition, which we were glad to do. All four of our children took a swing at learning to play it, and three of them actually did rather well. Amy, our youngest, stayed with it for many years and seemed to thoroughly enjoy it, as did I, hearing her play. Karen, our older daughter, also did well. In her early teens she bought the music to "Maple Leaf Rag," and learned to play it as a gift to her old musically challenged Dad. When Steve, our younger son, was in his first year of college and working some, he bought a used baby grand, and had it delivered on a Christmas day. It stayed in our house until he married. Later, when his family didn't have room for it, they rented it out for a while. When that episode played out, it came back to our house, to remain there for several more years. It came in handy for parties, especially those for our architectural office staff. Our long-time, faithful Secretary, Marilyn Weldin, is a trained and accomplished musician, having taught music in public schools earlier in her life. She would play Christmas carols and similar songs for us to sing, and others for us just to listen to.

My personal piano "talent" tops out with "Heart and Soul," and that thing, I don't know the name of, that you play by rolling your knuckles over the black keys, first one way and then the other. I can amuse my grandkids with this ability, as long as they are less than four years old. A few years later we donated that piano to a Spanish-speaking church.

The most listened to music in our house when I was growing up was simply called "Popular." Nowadays it is called "Big Band," or sometimes "Swing." It was intended for dancing, but my Baptist parents didn't do that. They probably didn't have any moral objections to it; they just didn't have any opportunities. When I got to my teens they had no problems with my going to dances, although I was so shy I refused to try to dance until I got to college. I would just hang around and sometimes be the disc jockey for the others, but that's another story.

If the piano was pretty much unconquerable, I was always open to the next challenge. The trumpet had always fascinated me; my image of it was somehow heroic and dashing. In the second semester of my freshman year in high school I signed up for the band. However, the only similar instrument available for me was a flugelhorn, in the same key as a trumpet, but mellower in tone. The scales are the same and I labored on diligently and generally enjoyed it, although I bristled a little because it wasn't a real trumpet.

After a while my folks found a used trumpet and bought it for me, a big ego-booster. After I gave up trying to play it my brother Allen took it up. He has the musical ear in the family. As he began to specialize in directing choral music, I retrieved it, and until recently still had it, beat up and tarnished as it was. Eventually I donated it to a drive for used instruments for the Nashville School System.

Often when I hear a nice trumpet piece, such as one of Purcell's, or one by a trumpet virtuoso like Wynton Marsalis, I find myself moistening my lips and puckering up, unconsciously, of course. My granddaughter, Erin, recently took it up. When she showed me her horn, to my dismay I found that I couldn't remember the scales. Now another grandchild, Ryan, has taken up the trumpet at his school.

If looking back my high school band interlude seems all too brief, it was not without it's moments. The regular practice time was after classes, about three o'clock each afternoon. One day Billy Campbell and I arrived about half an hour early for some reason. Billy had been playing trumpet for several years, maybe since sixth grade, and was an accomplished player, holding down first chair. No one else was there, and we sort of moseyed around, seeing that the music stands and chairs were all in place, but the only instruments out were the drums. Just to have something to do, I suppose, we went to a couple of snare drums and started to play marching cadences. I know I had never had any instruction on the drums, and I don't know if Billy had either, but we really got into it, just flailing away, joyfully. After a while the Director, Mr. Cowart, came in. He didn't stop us, just watched and listened. When we saw him we stopped, but he said, "Keep it up, that was great. Maybe you could help me teach some of the younger kids how to do that." I don't believe we ever did do any teaching, but it was a boost to my ego to hear that kind of praise.

When I was a Junior in high school a new radio station was built about a block from our house. I watched in fascination while the tower went up and the building took shape and the equipment was installed. I became a pest and hung around so much that the owners, the Dunnavant family, sort of took me in and let me pretend I was a part of the staff. They even let me have my own half hour record show for a while. I'm sure I was dreadful, but I thought I was hot stuff. What I played was the popular music of the day, by bands such as Tommy Dorsey, Glenn Miller, Benny Goodman, and Woody Herman.

Then, my freshman year in college some friends persuaded me to sign up for the proverbial "Music Appreciation" course as an elective. Everyone thought of it as easy credit, and so did I, because it really was easy for me. However it was more than that; it was delightful, for me almost an epiphany. I was introduced to "serious" music for the first time. It was explained to me and I've never looked back. I began to think of music as important, and took a serious interest in it. I even went on to take the follow-up course, "Fundamentals of Music" or some such, the next quarter.

Auburn had a program of visiting symphony orchestras, among other free events. I went to every one I could. These usually were held in a big old metal building, war surplus, I believe, called the Student Activities Building. One memorable concert was held in the winter. The building was heated by big gas-fired heaters hung overhead, and when they came on they created an awful racket, much to the annoyance of both musicians and audience. What was worse, though, occurred in the middle of a piece when the metal sides of the building began to expand from the heat and make very loud pops and cracks. The conductor became so enraged that he threw down his baton and stalked off the stage in a fury. He had to be coaxed back onstage and the heaters were turned off. It became very chilly by the end of the concert, but to my neophyte ears, the music was glorious.

There are many, perhaps thousands, of Alabama-born musicians of note. Probably the best place to check them out is a little-known but very fine museum, The Alabama Music Hall of Fame, in Tuscumbia. Though relatively small, its exhibits and archives are excellently presented, with a wide range of musical categories and types, from country to gospel, blues, swing and classical. Featured artists include Hank Williams, W. C. Handy, Tammy Wynette, and Aretha Franklin.

Speaking of W. C. Handy, his hometown is my beloved Florence. His home is now a house museum, and it is right in the middle of town. We used to drive by it at least once a week when I was a kid. I didn't know anything at all about his music, but knew he must have been important because Daddy seemed to be proud of the fact the Handy came from Florence. As far as I remember, his race was never mentioned.

While still in high school I enrolled in the church youth choir, and continued afterward, when home from college. I think I learned more about reading music from that experience than from playing in the band. I learned about timing from the differences in the way the notes are shown, and how they relate in pitch by where they fall on those five lines, whatever anyone calls them. What I could never master is recognizing the pitch, and which note was actually an A or B or whatever. In other words, I do not have an "ear" for music.

Because of the range of my voice, I have always tried to sing the bass line in church singing, and usually can. I sort of instinctively know what pitch comes next. A former Minister of Music in my church told me this is something like "feeling" the note, and I guess that just about describes it. I still enjoy singing in church; I try to make a "joyful noise." With some of the newer music I have a rather difficult time. One new practice that really bothers me is when the organist changes the harmonics, and the bass line isn't the way it's always been. It throws me and I often have to just stop trying. Don't these primadonnas realize the purpose of congregational music is to involve the congregation in the worship? And if we, the congregation, are thrown for a loop by their showing off then we can't participate with the joy and enthusiasm we would like to and should. No one should have to concentrate on the mechanics of the music because doing so keeps us from concentrating on its message.

My lack of a musical ear was only one of the reasons I never developed into a good trumpet player. Another is that I just couldn't reach the high notes. I seemed to do all right in the middle range, but pushing on up there was a real strain, and it sounded like it. My musical ability, such as it is, is mechanical, and not natural. Some people, and I admire them greatly, seem to just let the music "flow" from them; my daughter Amy, for example. I am amazed at the real musicians, and envy them, but I always enjoy hearing the gifted ones perform.

It has always seemed to me, at least since I became interested in music as a topic of its own, that there is a strong linkage between music and architecture. Parallel and similar structural concepts and rules. "Architecture is frozen music," is a quote frequently heard, attributed to both Schiller and Goethe. It doesn't much matter which; there is more than a whiff of truth in the thought. Many writers smarter than I have expounded on this idea, so I won't dwell on it, except to say that I find strength in it, and reinforcement of my convictions about architecture.

True, architecture may be thought of as "frozen"; it is static in physical terms, but if it truly is authentic architecture, it has the quality of movement, by moving those who experience it sensibly and emotionally. No one can just look at a really good and meaningful piece of architecture and not be affected in some way, and that experience can and perhaps should be called "moving." Sadly, too often what we like to call architecture does not meet this test, and fails in achieving authenticity.

An interesting and possibly instructive exercise for architecture students would be to link well-known buildings with well-known pieces of music. It might work this way, in a sort of seminar setting:

In a history of architecture class, after a survey of a meaningfully-clustered group of buildings, ask what "feelings" one might have when experiencing them, what do you think the designer wanted people to feel about them, and how well the designer succeeded. Then as the students view pictures of the buildings, play the selected music and ask them to match the music, and its emotive content, to the building. The objective would not be to arrive at any correct answers, only to open the student's minds to these ideas, and to encourage them to consider this aspect of thought in their design activity. If any architecture professors read this and want to use it in a class, be my guest.

5.

ATHENS

Two boll weevils grew up in Alabama. One went on to Hollywood and became a famous actor. The other stayed behind in the cotton fields and never amounted to much. The second one, naturally, became known as the lesser of two weevils.

Even though we had lived in Athens most of the summer of 1946, I had not made much progress in meeting new friends or otherwise becoming involved in the life of the town. Athens was and is smaller than Florence, and initially I felt it was somehow inferior. We did, though, immediately get involved in church, and I did meet people my age there, but I hadn't formed any fast friendships by the time school started in the fall. That was an especially stressful time. There I was, not quite fourteen, about as tall as I would ever be, and skinny as a pole. I weighed about 120 pounds. The typical anxieties of early teens weighed heavily on me, plus having to go to a new school where I knew practically no one.

Fortunately, it began to turn out all right rather quickly. I was sort of adopted by a group of kids who had known each other all their lives, and was made to feel right at home. This has been an immeasurable blessing, because those of us who are still around are very close to this day. We are life long friends who can call on each other for anything, even after all these years. There have been the usual reunions every five years or so. With great disappointment I missed the 50th; I was in the hospital with a quadruple heart by-pass. James Cobb, Boonie Hendricks Wiley, and I had worked hard on a booklet for this occasion. My office staff put it together. It was sent off to the reunion organizers, and then I didn't get to go! My classmates were very thoughtful and gracious, though. They sent well wishes galore. For several years a small group of the Class of '50 who live close enough meets in Athens once a quarter for breakfast. Nashville is less than one hundred miles from Athens and we are able to go some of the time.

If Florence was modeled after the Italian original, Athens is very much the prototypical southern county seat town in its make up and appearance. It has a central Court House Square, with the original street grid radiating out from that point. It is peppered with authentic antebellum houses, most occupied and in good repair. The older streets have sidewalks and broad verges of grass between sidewalk and curb, mature trees shading well-kept houses, a very civilized ambience. The stores and other buildings around the square are all of a scale and nicely define the space, the way urban places should.

When I was a teenager the pavement around the square was brick, and a little rough to drive over. It has since been replaced with conventional asphalt paving, which to my mind is a loss. The bricks were a civilizing element because they forced drivers to slow down and be more aware of their surroundings, and if you are more aware, you tend to care more. One cold January night I had use of the family car, a 1941 Ford two-door sedan, and was returning home about one AM after a date. It was below freezing and there was a glaze of ice on the bricks. When I drove through the square I had to make a turn and, due to the ice on the street, I went into a spin, and made about one and a half turns before stopping. There was no one else around and I thought that was so much fun that I drove around the block and purposively spun out again.

I lived in Athens in a full-time way for only two periods, my high school years and the seventeen months between leaving the Air Force and going back to college, but the first of those was extremely meaningful and important to my development. I suppose the teen years are that way for everyone. In my case there were many positives. Because the school was small, I was able to try my hand at many things that probably would not be possible for today's students in large schools. My children and grandchildren appear to have been more limited in the opportunities and options of things to become involved in compared to those available to those of us at good old Athens High.

The war created many heroes for the nation, for all Americans, and especially for an impressionable youth like myself. Sometime shortly after we moved to Athens I got the idea of collecting autographs from some of these men, and I wrote to them, asking for their autographs. These included President Harry Truman, Generals Eisenhower and Marshall, Admirals Halsey and Nimitz, J. Edgar Hoover, and Henry Ford. Surprisingly, I received responses to all of my letters, but only a few of the requested autographs. I actually got two autographs from Eisenhower, who at the time was President of Columbia University. One was on a business card, and another on a letter sending the card. Others I received were from Halsey, Nimitz, and Hoover. Truman's Secretary wrote saying that the President regretted that he couldn't reply. Ford's office sent a similar letter. I was still very proud of my collection. Unfortunately, it disappeared sometime while I was in college. These autographs might have been worth a tidy sum today.

In the spring of my freshman year I took up the trumpet and joined the band. I stayed with this, marching and playing not only at football games but also in parades at such stellar events as the annual Strawberry Festival in Cullman, Alabama, until football spring practice began in 1948. Daddy had played football in his high school, and I wanted to do the same. I stuck with that the rest of my high school years. Although I was never very good at it, I enjoyed the camaraderie and just the exuberance of trying something rather difficult, at least strenuous. My problem with athleticism, or lack thereof, is that I just couldn't catch the ball. I could do most other things reasonably well, but my size limited me, and I was relegated to the position of defensive end. Fortunately, for me at least, there were not enough people in school to turn away any willing body, so I got to play.

At a larger school, no doubt I would not have gotten to play much, if at all. In those days it was not uncommon for a small school team to play the both ways, offense and defense, but I was so bad at catching the ball that I was allowed to play defense only. Apparently I did that fairly well for someone of my size. In addition, I went out for basketball and for track, but I just didn't have what it took, and soon dropped out of both.

I earned an athletic letter in my senior year, being inducted into the "A" Club. The initiation was rather bizarre. We went through some silly stunts for a couple of hours on initiation night, and as a finale were taken out into the county some seven or eight miles, set free, and left to walk home. The only humiliating thing occurred at the official induction, which took place on the stage in the gym at an assembly before the whole student body. Each new member had to sit in a chair, and a girl, usually his current girlfriend or whomever he happened to date last, came up and shaved his head. Needless to say, the skill the girls exhibited in cutting hair was rather limited, or perhaps downright mean-spirited, and all of us who had been sheared went to the barbershop afterward to get things smoothed out into a more presentable form. One of my photos in the yearbook was taken right after this august event, and my head is almost as bare as Michael Jordan's.

We had class plays in both our Junior and Senior years, and, guess what, I was in both, although not in starring roles. I wrote for our weekly school newspaper, the <u>Scan-it.</u> I worked on my Senior Class yearbook, the <u>Aquila.</u> The school mascot was (is) a golden eagle; Aquila is Latin for eagle. I did some of the page layouts, illustrations, and other graphic things, including caricatures of the entire faculty, some seventeen in all. That shows how big a school it was then.

My writing for the school newspaper was perhaps natural; by this time Mama had started to work at one of the two local weeklies, first as a bookkeeper, but gradually doing other things, taking photos of social events and then writing the social column. Eventually she became the Society Editor. From my earliest memory Mama drilled us, my brothers and me, in proper grammar. Not that she gave us lessons at home, she just corrected us severely if we misused a word or used poor grammar in any way. I still don't remember all the nitty-gritty, but I usually recognize mistakes, and try to avoid them. I continued to write sporadically all through high school and college, on rare occasions getting published, never getting paid until much later, and then very little.

Later on, the two papers merged, and still later, the survivor began daily publication. Mama stayed on and at some point started writing a column named "Orr-Bits." I guess that shows where my penchant for puns comes from.

Our Principal at Athens High School was Mr. Julian Newman. Among the students he had a reputation for gruffness, but we all knew he was fair and wanted the best for all of us. He showed this on more than one occasion. One directly affected me.

No one could have been more surprised than I when on the first day of our second semester of my freshman year Bobby Raney showed up. I had known Bobby in Florence, and his family had moved to Athens over the Christmas holidays. His father and an uncle owned a chain of jukeboxes and vending machines placed in various towns around North Alabama and Middle Tennessee. We soon renewed the friendship we had enjoyed in Florence.

Not surprisingly, sometime in our sophomore year Bobby and I began to have a heightened interest in cars, and decided that we would like to be automobile mechanics. One way to do this, to get the training we would need, was to enroll in what was called "Diversified Occupations," or D. O., which was a cooperative program where the students go to class half the day and work in a commercial facility the other half, learning the trade. When we went to Mr. Newman and tried to apply for the D. O. program, he wouldn't let us, telling us that the D. O. program was for students who are not likely to go to college, and that excluded the two of us. He was right, of course. Bobby went on to college and had a long successful career with Monsanto. Our friendship remained strong. Bobby was one of my groomsmen in our wedding.

On another occasion I was in a casual conversation with Mr. Newman about my future plans. I told him I thought I would like to be an architect, but I was afraid that the field was too crowded. Part of that fear was due to Daddy's thought that architecture was a dying field. Mr. Newman told me that there is always room at the top. While I never reached "the top," I have had a very meaningful and fulfilling career in architecture, and am grateful to Mr. Newman for his encouragement.

There was an organization at Athens High School named the "Tuberculosis Projection Club," or TBPC, of which I was a member. We took a 16mm movie projector around to other schools, all, if I remember correctly, out in the county, not city schools, and showed two old black and white films on the perils of, and therapies for, TB. One of the attractions was that we got to skip school to do this, but maybe we did some good. They gave us neat little enamel lapel pins for our service. I still have mine somewhere. One collateral benefit to me from this experience came some years later when I was in the Air Force. I'll tell about that later.

My first conscious interest in architecture as a future career came during my high school years, actually pretty early. When my family joined First Baptist Church in Athens soon after moving from Florence, we learned that they were planning a new building, relocating to a new site across the street. One evening service the schematic plans were presented by the architect, Tom Gardner, from Nashville. I was captivated, realizing that this was something I might be able to do, and would like to do. I never spoke to Mr. Gardner, but I followed the progress of the project eagerly and diligently. I watched the building go up, identifying all the materials and how they fit together, carefully observing, trying to understand why some things were done the way they were. Aside from a few new houses, this was the first time I had been able to see how all of this worked together to produce in the end a complete building. Maybe my fascination with it was partly because by then I was old enough to grasp it all in a comprehensive way.

I have always liked to draw; put more succinctly, I have always felt a *compulsion* to draw. Mama tried me out on coloring books as early as most kids see them, in my preschool years. I didn't do too well; I didn't like to stay inside the lines, and Mama didn't like that. I didn't think that was as important as creating something I liked more. In later years Mama and I had disagreements about this same idea when she tried to get my kids to color between the lines and I said leave them alone to do what they wanted. Finally I just banned coloring books from the house and gave the kids the blank back sides of unused specification pages from the office for them to draw on.

By my teen years I realized that I had some kind of creative streak in me, continually feeling the need to come up with new "things" I could show in drawings, and in other ways. I liked to try to make things, especially things that hadn't existed before. I remember when I was five I made a toy tank with a length of 2 X 4 about a foot long. I nailed the bell from an alarm clock on top for the turret, tapped a large nail on the front for a cannon, and nailed on bottle caps for wheels. The father of a friend asked where I got it and he didn't believe me when I said I had made it. My dad finally had to confirm to him that I really did make it. One way this creative urge might be said to have originated would be in a heightened imagination. My mother told me years later, that when I was very young she and Daddy feared I would grow up to be a criminal or worse because I had such an imagination that at times it seemed that I was destined to be the world's greatest liar. I hope I don't give that impression now, but because of my perverse sense of humor it may be difficult to tell the difference sometimes.

My Uncle Paul McClinton, my Aunt Eugenia's husband, had a shop in his garage with a full array of power tools and other gear, and he made all kinds of fascinating stuff. They lived in Birmingham and I loved to visit him and just hang around in his shop. He subscribed to Popular Mechanics, Popular Science, and Mechanics Illustrated, and he gave me copies of some of them after he had read them. They inspired me to believe I could make the kinds of things I saw in them. The negative side was that I didn't like to keep at anything very long. I was impatient and would quickly tire of it. I started untold numbers of model airplane kits, never to really finish even one. One of those magazines had a column for aspiring inventors. You could write in with an idea for an invention and an Editor would publish the letter, with a reply, telling the "inventor" what he thought about it. I had an idea for a toy bowling alley, using pins with cords with weights on them attached to the bottoms, going through holes in the bottom of the alley. A board under the alley would hold the weights up when someone bowled, but would drop down when it was time to reset the pins, pulling the pins back upright. The Editor didn't seem to think much of my invention.

Although I had been driving since I was thirteen, and on my own much of the time, I didn't have a car I could use anytime I wanted. Fortunately I had friends who did. One drove a war surplus Jeep, and several of us would pile into it after school in good weather and just ride around. In cold months he would drive a 1941 Ford, cramming seven or eight of us in it. I have seen so many in the front seat that the driver actually sat second from the driver's side door. One time nephew, about four at the time, unintentionally set fire to the car and burned up much of the interior. For some reason the front seat didn't burn. The car was still drivable, and we rode around in it like it was, a burned out shell. The rear window was gone, and someone could and sometimes did sit on the shelf under the window, feet inside and upper body out in the wind. Eventually they got it repaired.

I suppose that my teens were not a lot different from others of that time. I went through all the typical anxieties. I fell in love with several girls who wouldn't give me a thought. I dated as much as I could, but was limited by having to use the family car, and meager funds. I was no Romeo. Mostly I just had a good time.

The summer between my Junior and Senior years might have been momentous- might have been, but wasn't. My close friend, James Cobb, had an older brother whom I had never met. He had left home and moved to Texas before my family moved to Athens. Through contacts with him, James arranged before school was out for the two of us to go out to Texas and work in the wheat harvest, following it from the Texas fields, through the plains states all the way to Canada. My folks agreed that this was a practical thing. In later years they permitted my brother Johnny to go with a group of teen-aged boys from Athens up to Ohio to de-tassel corn on large agricultural tracts. I believe he did that two summers while he was in high school. My folks were open to their sons being allowed to try new and different things as part of the growing up process.

Mama was out shopping shortly before James and I were to leave, looking for some appropriate work clothes for me and other things I might need for the summer. She happened to meet Mrs. Cobb, and asked her what she thought about work clothes for the "boys."

Unfortunately for our plans in general, and for James in particular, this was the first time Mrs. Cobb had heard of this proposed adventure. That quashed the whole thing in short order, and we went on to another routine summer. Maybe it was a good thing. I have what are sometimes severe nasal allergies, which might have sent me packing early, working around all that chaff and such.

My contemporaries either saw something creative in me, or saw me as a sap they could dump any difficult job onto. I'd like to think it was the former. I enjoyed doing new stuff. My senior year I was put in charge of decorating the gym for the Prom, and what I came up with was perhaps my first architectural construction. Let's see if I can describe it. We pieced together five long strips of wood, as long as the gym itself, and strung cords across them every few inches. We wove strips of crepe paper through the cords, in colored bands resembling the rainbow, making a canopy. We lifted the center and the next two outboard strips up toward the ceiling with cords, through the light fixtures. What we made had a cross section like a barn, but a very colorful one. It was quite a hit. That is what I remember of the Prom. I don't even remember if I had a date or not, probably not. Apparently no pictures of this survive.

That year I also applied for a Naval ROTC scholarship, and to my great surprise was accepted. As I have mentioned, my grades were not all that spectacular. Regardless, there I was, committed to this path.

Graduation came, without much excitement. I don't remember much about it, but one episode I do remember. The night of graduation a party was held at Barbara Hurn's house. We didn't do anything very outrageous. If any drinking was done, I didn't see it; we lived in a dry county and never saw much evidence of drinking by our crowd. We just danced and visited like teenagers did in those long-ago days. After staying up almost all night three of us left to go to a next-day all-day party at someone's "Camp" on the lake. The "Lake" in this case is a stretch of the Elk River very close to where it meets the Tennessee, where the water is backed up by Wheeler Dam, just a few miles downstream. The river is quite wide there, and many families have camps along the banks, varying from primitive cabins to rather large and nicely appointed homes. All have boat docks.

Highway US 72 crosses the Elk east to west, with the east end much higher above the water than the west, and we used to go swimming there, jumping off into the river, maybe 40 or 50 feet above the water. As far as I know no one was ever hurt doing this.

The site of our party was a typical camp, a rather rustic house and a boat dock. The three of us arrived slightly before dawn, and having nothing else to do, decided to go swimming. There were no others around, so wearing bathing suits was not required. I had one and put it on, but the others didn't. We found an inflated rubber boat, and went into the water with it, paddling around a while. Having been up all night we soon began to get sleepy, and dozed off, draped across the boat. We awoke an hour or so later, and found that we had drifted with the current downstream at least a mile. That's when we realized that we had no paddles. We began to paddle furiously with our hands, and finally, after an hour or so of strenuous effort, arrived back at the camp, only to find that everyone else was there. The other two quickly dived into the water to preserve their modesty, while I swam ashore and swam back out with their clothes. All three of us were rather badly sunburned, they in some awkward and uncomfortable places.

That summer I worked in a new "chicken-plucking" plant, the Beasley Bailey Poultry Co. Also working there were James Cobb and another classmate, Bobby "Stink" Wood. This company processed chickens, from being trucked in alive, to being killed, cleaned, packed in ice, and shipped out to retailers. The three of us worked on the packing and delivery end. I got to drive a truck to Nashville and Birmingham regularly delivering them. It was a great time for a seventeen year old.

One day our immediate boss, a fellow named Rockhill, came in and rather dramatically said, "Gentlemen, we are at war!" He was referring to the Korean War, of course. It was the summer of 1950. Almost immediately every semi-adult male became fodder for the draft. One of the first National Guard units to be mobilized was from Athens, an engineering battalion. Many Athens boys went down to enlist in the Guard, preferring to go to war with some people they knew if they were going to have to go at all, and because of the draft, just about any male between the ages of seventeen and forty, with

Alabama Boy

two good legs, would be going. Since I had been accepted into the NROTC program I didn't have that threat hanging over me, but a lot of others did. Stink and James signed up with the Guard and soon left the job. James was found to have some sort of medical condition that kept him out of the Army, but Stink went in and served in Korea. I worked at Beasley Bailey for parts of the next two summers, before or after my required summer NROTC cruises.

After returning from Korea, Stink attended Florence State College, since renamed the University of North Alabama, in Florence, on a football scholarship, playing for Coach Hal Self, who had coached at Athens High for our sophomore and Junior years. Stink had a successful business career in Athens, and served as Mayor for four years. James attended and played football at Abilene Christian College in Texas, and stayed in Texas for most of his working life.

In high school I had had a variety of other jobs in Athens. The first regular job- meaning it went on week after week- was at the A&P grocery. I worked there on Saturdays only for several months. At that time the family still had the last car Daddy had bought before WWII, the old 1941 Ford. It had picked up a lot of minor dings and scrapes, but still drove just fine. One Saturday morning Mama dropped me off at the store, and a coworker who witnessed my arrival, noticing the battered condition, asked me, "How many people learned to drive in that car?" I had to admit, only one, me, but Mama had done some of the damage.

I also worked in a variety store, two different men's clothing stores, a small department store and the Post Office. Mostly these were during the summer or over the Christmas holidays, and sometimes just on Saturdays. I remember one cold, dreary, rainy Saturday in February in the men's store. My only coworker was an elderly fellow named Charlie Hill. Charlie was a jolly sort with a great sense of humor. By about mid-afternoon we had had practically no one even come into the store, and Charlie asked me, "What kind of day have you been having?"

"I haven't sold a thing," I said, "how about you?"

He replied, "I had one thirty-nine cent sale and a whole bunch of little ones."

I have often remembered this little episode, taking it as a reminder to always do the best job I could, even when it might seem to be unimportant and insignificant.

I've always appreciated folks who enjoy humor, and Charlie certainly did.

My class at Athens High School graduated in 1950, and celebrated our 50th reunion in 2000. Only 58 strong, some of us felt that graduating in the mid-century year made us a little special. Years have shown that we have fared no better nor worse than similar groups. However, we have never lost our optimism or our sense of responsibility to try to make the world better.

In preparation for our reunion, we sent all surviving members a questionnaire asking for information on family, careers, hobbies, civil service, and the like. The responses were assembled into booklets and distributed to all class members. The last question reads:

"As a member of the Class of 1950, what advice would you like to give to the Class of 2000?"

Here are some of the responses:

- Look at the bright side.

- Stay in school. Get as much education as you can. Try to help others.

- Wherever you go, stay in touch with your church, family and friends. They will be your support when things go wrong and will make success sweeter by sharing your joy.

- Know who you are. Put God first and wisely make life-choices: mate, vocation, friends, activities, and interests. Exercise a positive attitude about yourself and other people. Give your best and enjoy your choices. Keep priorities in order.

- Proverbs 3:4-6 "If you want favor with both God and man, and a reputation for good judgment and common sense, then trust the Lord completely; don't ever trust yourself. In everything you do, put God first, and He will direct you and crown your efforts with success." (Living Bible, paraphrased)

- ALWAYS REMEMBER:

  1. Be the first to forgive.
  2. To waste time is to waste life itself.
  3. People are more important than things.
  4. Never allow a financial interest to crush a moral principle.
  5. Happiness is a habit. Cultivate it.
  6. Always put God first in your life and show honor also to your country.

- The government does not owe you a living. If a man will not work, neither let him eat.

- Take being a member of the class of 2000 as a special endowment and responsibility to lead the world to a better place. Believe in the goodness of others. Believe in yourself. Never, never compromise integrity. Live ethically.

- Shape up!

Our intention was limited to possibly sharing these with the graduating class of our alma mater. Perhaps all class of 2000 graduates will find them worth pondering.

Daddy had always had Fords, believing that they were better suited to rural stresses; Chevrolets were supposed to be "town" cars. After the War his first car was not a Ford. I'm not sure why. I guess he thought it was a good idea at the time. It was a Nash two-door sedan, a huge tank of a car by today's standards, and seriously underpowered. It had so much space between the front seat and the dashboard that we joked that if we wanted we had room to put in a row of chairs there, and not crowded the other seats. It also had front doors that must have been at almost six feet wide. One day Daddy pulled up and parked parallel to the curb, and swung the door open without looking. Another car came along just then and just took the door right out of his hand and off the car. After that he had Fords again the rest of his life.

Athens holds sad memories as well. In 1959 Daddy died from a heart attack. He was baby-sitting for Nancy and me with Mark, our first, listening to an Auburn basketball game on the radio, when he had his first symptoms. Later that night, Allen, who was eighteen years old then, called and told us that Daddy had been taken to the hospital. He died ten days later of a second attack, on Valentine's Day. Johnny was attending Union University in Jackson, Tennessee, on a basketball scholarship. Nancy and I were there in Jackson visiting him and his wife Mary at this time, when his coach came to the house and told us that Daddy had died.

It was devastating for all of us. Daddy was well known in town and many friends and acquaintances attended the funeral. Anyone who has been personally involved in a family funeral, especially in the south, knows that the practice of friends bringing food to the family as a show of love and concern is just one of those "has to" things. We were blessed with such an abundance that was almost embarrassing. But, it showed how much Daddy was admired, and how much the community cared for our family. It was humbling.

Being the strong person she was Mama soon pulled herself together and got on with her life, as did we all. Because of his age, and being single, Allen was perhaps affected more deeply than Johnny or I. He became the "man of the house" and filled that role admirably. Life, though, moved on.

6.

FOOD

In our house the three major food groups were fried chicken, green beans and mashed potatoes.

*A*s I shared in the last chapter, food is vitally important for more than mere nutrition, in times of grief as well as in times of joy.

I'll admit that Alabama food is about the same as any other Southern food, but its what I grew up with, and that's how I thought about it. In my childhood and teens at home, food was rather predictable, wholesome but a little dull. We always had cereal, scrambled eggs, bacon, and toast for breakfast, and what we would now call "meat and three" for supper, either roast beef, fried chicken, ham, or pork chops, with the usual veggies. The evening meal was "Supper"; "Dinner" was the mid-day meal. I suspect this was the norm in many homes all across the country.

When we lived on Beulah Avenue in Florence, our next-door neighbors, the Rodens, had a cow, and we bought milk from them. Mr. Roden was a barber and we went to his shop for our haircuts most of the time. There were five sons and two daughters in the Roden family, the girls being roughly the same ages as Johnny and me. All five of the boys served in WWII. In the summer Mr. Roden and the boys would set up washtubs in their back yard and make sauerkraut, and the smell wafted through the neighborhood wonderfully. I don't suppose that kraut would be considered a typical Alabama dish, but I can't help but think of it as such.

"Dinner" varied depending on whether it was a school day or not. The typical school "dinner," especially at Gilbert School, was wieners, baked beans, and sauerkraut, served in a tin plate. The drink was milk served in a small glass bottle with a cardboard stopper, just like the quart size bottles we had at home. Sometimes we had chocolate milk. I'm sure there was some variety, but this is the only menu I remember. In higher grades the food was typical school cafeteria fare, certainly with nothing like the choices kids have today.

Grits always have always been, and remain today, a mainstay of Southern eating, especially for breakfast. However, it wasn't so at our house. Daddy explained this anomaly one day. He said that when he went off to college at Auburn, grits were served for breakfast every day, no matter where a student chose to eat. He got so sick of grits that he swore he would "never eat another grit in his life." When I went to Auburn, that had not changed, but perhaps because I hadn't been burned out on them at home, I sort of liked them. At least I didn't dislike them; there really was more variety available then.

When I was in the first grade, Daddy bought me 100 baby chicks to raise. We had a small chicken house and fenced in yard at the rented house where we lived at the time. The idea was that I would take care of them, feeding them, changing the water, etc. and what we didn't eat ourselves we would sell, and I would get the money. Being a poultry husbandry specialist, he no doubt thought that this was a good way to indoctrinate me into the family vocational specialty. Well, I tried, but probably not very hard, and it was just another bit of evidence that I wasn't cut out for agriculture in any form. Some of the chicks died, possibly from neglect. Some grew to frying size and we killed, dressed, cooked, and ate them. Maybe there were a few that we sold for profit; I don't remember. At any rate, we ate chicken a lot, homegrown or bought elsewhere.

Another meat we had often was pork chops. They were almost inedible. Mama had grown up on a farm where hogs were raised. A serious disease known as trichinosis could be contracted from their meat. The process of curing ham got rid of the problem, but uncured meat, such as pork chops, was dangerous if not cooked to a crisp. Pork chops at our house tended to be about as thick as the sole of a dress shoe, and just as tough. All the taste had been cooked out of them. I didn't know till I left home that pork chops didn't have to be this way, and could be tender and tasty. Today's meat processing technology has virtually removed the threat of trichinosis. Pork chops are a treasured fixture in Southern cooking to this day.

However, one quintessential way of preparing and serving pork remains strong in the south, with an important Alabama connection, and that is barbeque. Apparently in the world of barbeque, pork is king east of the Mississippi River, and beef out west. One of the most popular brands of pork barbeque in the south is Whitt's. What gives this fact its particular importance to me is that the Whitt's brand originated in my home town of Athens, Alabama, with the family of people I was in school with. When our large family of four children, in-laws, grandchildren and often friends gather we almost always buy four or so pounds of Whitt's and assorted side dishes. In our unbiased opinion it can't be beat.

There is an apocryphal tale about the origin of one of the favorite desserts of Alabama. It seems that in the days when just about all middle income households in Alabama had what was euphemistically called "Help," an African American lady who cleaned and cooked and raised the babies, etc. there was one such home in which this conversation took place:

> "My, this is delicious pie, Bessie!" said the lady of the house. " What kind of pie is it? What do you call it?"
>
> Bessie replied, "Oh, ma'am, its Chess Pie." (Corruption of "Just" pie).

True or not, this illustrates that pies are essential to Alabama thinking about desserts. In my childhood we had apple pie more often that any other, with mincemeat a close second. Often it would be served with a slice of cheese melted over the top and a scoop of ice cream on top of that. Mama could make ice cream in the freezer section of the refrigerator, using an ice tray with the ice cube dividers removed. It wouldn't be much, just enough for a small serving for each of us. Of course, we had an ice cream freezer, the kind you had to crank for what seemed to be hours, and got a sore arm, before it was ready. We almost always had vanilla, and to this day I tend to think of ice cream as vanilla, and any other flavor as something else, and usually something inferior.

Like many Alabama homemakers, Mama was used to doing things in the home, even though she almost always had an outside job. About every mother I knew anything about "put up" jellies and preserves. I have never understood the difference between jam and preserves, but in our part of the world it was always called preserves. Another, and perhaps unique, skill Mama had was making pickles. She prepared the cucumbers, cleaning them and cutting them up in the desired forms, and steeped them in brine in a large earthen churn for several weeks. I suspect they were the only pickles I tasted until I was in high school, and I thought they were delicious.

There is a food product unique to the middle South – sorghum syrup. Most of the time it is simply called "Sorghum." This is made from the sorghum cane, and is similar to sugar cane, but, its supporters claim, is tastier and more nutritious. My Uncle Louie grew it on his farm, and we used to go out and watch when it was time to harvest it. Daddy would cut off short pieces of cane, peel them, and give them to us to chew on, sucking the sweet juice out. We spit out the fiber. It isn't edible.

The syrup was made by feeding the stalks into a mill, which on my uncle's farm was driven by a mule, hitched to long pole, going around in circles. As the juice is squeezed out, it is collected in vats, and then boiled down to get the syrup. The color is darker than cane syrup, and the taste a little sharper. It has more tang to it. It is delicious.

It can be eaten several ways, many the same as you would cane or maple syrup, but one the special ways is to pour some in a plate or saucer, mix in a little butter, and take biscuits, broken into halves, and place them down in the mixture, browned side up. You eat them with fork. Enjoy!

Like many other aspects of our lives, food has become more universal and common. I never heard of pizza until Jack Ibach, one of my college roommates, from Baldwin, Long Island, New York, told me about it. I wasn't real sure what he was talking about, and it was still later that I actually tasted one. Think how common they are today. Much of traditional southern food, at least the way it has usually been cooked, is not very healthy, and we have strayed away from it. However, McDonald's is not very healthy, either. Maybe we've swapped one bad practice for another, one with less cultural meaning, further diluting our heritage.

Maybe a good way to conclude this chapter is with the recipe for what is probably a standard for kids and grownup kids all over the world. My wife, Nancy, an Alabama girl, invented it and I recorded it. I call it her "Killer Peanut Butter and Jelly Sandwich," and it goes like this:

> On a small plate place two heaping tablespoons of peanut butter, smooth or crunchy to your choice. Add an equal amount of jelly or jam, flavor of choice, and a generous portion of butter or oleo. If desired, substitute honey for the jam or jelly. With a fork stir vigorously, until arriving at a smooth and homogenous mixture.
>
> Select your bread, white or wheat, but rye or pumpernickel probably would not be good choices. Spread this gooey mixture evenly on the bread. It likely will be enough for about six normal sandwiches, but normal is not operable here. Make it fit two, leaving a layer about one half inch thick. As you bite into it the mixture will ooze out around the edges. Do not be disturbed. This is part of the experience. Just lick the excess off around the edges as you go.
>
> As they say in LA (Lower Alabama), "Bon Appetite, you all!"

7.

BREAKING AWAY

Like Tevye, Isaac was a milkman in old Russia. He delivered his milk in a two-wheeled pushcart. One day a spoke broke in one of the wheels. Not having time to repair it before making his rounds, he resorted instead to using a wheelbarrow, causing the milk to churn around so much that it all curdled. This led to that old Russian saying:

"Where there's a wheel there's whey."

Going to college was never a question for my brothers and me; we would go. Where we went was only slightly less certain. The obvious first choice would be Auburn. I didn't have any objection to that, having been thoroughly indoctrinated since birth to its superiority over any other possibility. Johnny, being the "jock" of the three of us, attended Union University in Jackson, Tennessee, on a basketball scholarship. Allen attended Auburn for his undergraduate degree, and went on to a masters' degree at Southern Baptist Theological Seminary in Louisville, Kentucky, and a doctorate in anthropology at Columbia University in New York. I'm very proud of both of them.

What I preferred to study, though, fell into a rather narrow range of options. Because as long as I could remember I had doodled, sketched, drawn ideas for cars, buildings, inventions of various kinds, my field of study had to be something very "creative," in the visual arts arena. I began to think about a career in architecture, and as high school graduation approached and a decision about my future loomed, I was convinced that this was the right choice for me. Given his practical life view though, Daddy had different ideas. He was convinced that architecture was a dying field, and that engineering would be a better choice. In the Auburn catalog we found what seemed at the time to be a sensible compromise, Industrial Design. In this field things produced by industry were designed, such as cars, appliances, etc. Reluctantly, I agreed and signed on as a freshman in Industrial Design in the fall of 1950.

Throughout our life together my relations with Daddy were somewhat strained. Obviously, there was love, but often there was not real understanding. He was a self-made man, who always looked at the practical first, and maybe rarely at anything else. Our brains were just not wired the same way, although neither of us knew how to express that in those days. He was practical; I am creative. In architectural parlance he was rational; I am intuitive. Today we would say that he was a left-brain person; I am a right brainer. None of this should be taken that I do not value him or what he stood for in any way. He taught me much that has gone into who I am, and what I believe and stand by. It is not a tragedy that we were so different. It is only that the differences sometimes made for difficult times, but we got through them.

Paying for college, though, was not a certainty. I'm sure my parents would have found a way to finance college for me and my brothers, but in my case it proved to be not necessary, at least for the basic expenses of tuition, books, room and board.

During my senior year at Athens High School I came across the Naval ROTC program, and applied and was accepted. At the time there was only one college in each state with this program, although it has been expanded since then, and fortunately Auburn was and is still a designated institution in Alabama for the NROTC program. The program offered two tracks. One is a partial scholarship, paralleling the benefits and requirements found in the Army and Air Force ROTC programs. It is called the "Contract" program. The other, called the "Regular" program, is a full scholarship, providing direct payment for tuition, books, uniforms, etc., and a monthly stipend for room and board. Students in both options of the program were called Midshipmen, same as those at the Naval Academy. All men, and in those days it was only men, in both options went to the same ROTC classes and twice-weekly drills. The major difference was that the scholarship midshipmen were obligated to go on summer "cruises" all three summers in a four-year college career, and contract midshipmen only went on the last of those, the one between the junior and senior years.

The word "cruise" could be a little misleading. The first and third are actual cruises on warships to various exotic places, spending time learning miscellaneous Naval things. Those of us from NROTC units were placed alongside midshipmen from the Naval Academy, with no differences in how we were treated. The second cruise, however, was primarily on land, except for the time we spent in the air. More on this later.

I had jumped into college life eagerly, feeling simultaneously important and overwhelmed. In those days there were rather rigid proscriptions imposed on freshmen, called "Rats." We had to attend all pep rallies, and all home football games, and most daunting of all, we, at least the males, had to wear a "Rat Cap," a blue and orange beanie, at all times. If an upperclassman caught a freshman without one there could be unspecified penalties assessed, such as so many pushups, or some such idiocy. Fortunately, the student body was large enough that if one were alert and quick it was possible to avoid being identified as a freshman, at least most of the time. One planned indignity in the fall quarter was a foot race, called the "Rat Race," for all freshmen men. Fraternities and dorms sponsored teams and individuals, and prizes were awarded. I was not in a fraternity at that time, nor did I live in a dorm, so I skipped it and went to a movie. I don't remember which, but it was the fall of 1950, so that might narrow it down for movie buffs.

Football had always been a passion of mine, and continues to this day, so having to attend all home games didn't seem to be much of a burden, at least at first. The costs of the tickets were included in our fees. My freshman year of 1950 was the worst football season in Auburn history; the Tigers won not a single game. Nevertheless, I attended loyally. I especially remember one game, with Wofford. The temperature was about fifty degrees when the game started, and the stadium was comfortably if not completely filled, since it looked like we might beat this "breather" opponent. Sometime during the first half the wind picked up from the north and rapidly increased in velocity and decreased the temperature. By the time the middle of the fourth quarter rolled around the temperature could not have been over twenty degrees, and I doubt that there were more than 200 people left in the stands. A buddy and I stuck it out, though, only to see Auburn fall in defeat, 19 to 14.

The next season we got a new coach, the legendary Ralph "Shug" Jordan, and a new and more glorious football era began.

There were no standardized tests, such as the SAT or ACT when I was in high school. We did have some sort of tests, I remember, probably similar to those, given in both the junior and senior years. We weren't told what they were for, exactly, and were not told how we did. I wonder to this day what they were supposed to accomplish. However, when I got to Auburn we were given a series of placement tests, to determine whether we should be placed in standard, remedial or advanced classes. Math was never a strong suit with me, so I was not surprised that I was put in a remedial algebra class. I didn't think of myself as a whiz in English either, but to my surprise I was placed in an advanced English class. I blame this on Mama's hard-nosed attitude toward correct grammar, which she drilled into us almost daily. There seemed to be too many assigned to the remedial math classes, so a couple of weeks after classes started several of us were pulled out and sent to a new class, with what appeared to be an accelerated program.

I was also enrolled in English literature, history, economics, and PE, as well as the beginning courses in the Industrial Design program and the NROTC classes. One lesson I learned in that fall quarter was to never, never sign up for an eight o'clock class. That's when I had Economics 101, and I struggled to stay awake through it, dozing off practically every day. Luckily, I squeaked by and passed, if just barely. I was able to avoid ever scheduling another eight o'clock class the rest of my college career.

For the first two years all male students had to be in one of the ROTC programs, unless physically impaired. This meant classes and drills, which sometimes were actual close order marching drills, but more often, at least for those of us in NROTC, they were training sessions in gunnery, shipboard hardware, and the like.

Another requirement for the first two years was Physical Education, or PE. For men, the classes were organized into six areas, and everyone had to take a course in each of the six, covering the first two years. The first was a universal course, the same for everyone. After that each area had three or so options. I don't remember all of the areas or the choices, but I do recall some. One was Track and Field, and I chose track. Another area was called Gymnastics, and my choice was apparatus. I was only so-so in both these courses. The third I remember was called Combative, and the options were boxing, wrestling and fencing. I didn't take to the idea of having someone hitting me, or grappling around with another sweaty male, so I picked fencing, and thoroughly enjoyed it. The fourth was Team Sports. I don't remember what the Team Sport choices were but I took basketball.

The fifth was Aquatics. My course seems in retrospect to have been a general swimming overview. I knew how to swim, of course; in fact I can't remember when I couldn't swim. When we lived in Florence the family very often went swimming at a large pool located next to the county fair grounds. These were great times for me and for all of us, even Mama, who never learned to swim. At Auburn, swimming was taught in the college pool, a tiny thing located on the Ground Floor of the original gym, which had long since been abandoned for anything other than intramural volleyball. A much larger and better-equipped gym had been built for the varsity and for PE classes in basketball, gymnastics, fencing, and other such. The "Old Gym" would be torn down not long after that and replaced with a new Student Center Building. The swimming pool was about the size of a volleyball court, with side lines about three feet wide. Our instructor was a WWII veteran; there were a lot of them around then; named Archie something or other. He and I were to meet years later which I'll tell about then.

I did not make sterling grades in any of the PE courses, but you know, I got by, not having to repeat any of them.

The Industrial Design, or ID, program was in the School of Architecture and the Arts, under the administration of the Art Department. That meant that the early courses were standard art courses, such as freehand drawing, and a course called Basic Design. These I ate up. Later courses in this line included watercolor painting and printmaking. Other support courses in the Industrial Design curriculum, taken later, included shop courses, taught in the engineering school, such as woodworking, metalworking and welding. These were very interesting, giving me a broad background in understanding the processes of production of building materials and systems very useful in my future practice of architecture. The ID courses had two components, typical lectures and what were called Labs, which were similar to Studio courses in architecture, on drawing boards and building models, etc. I soon became mildly enthusiastic about all of this, and generally of all my courses (excepting math and economics). Another benefit that the ID experience brought to me in my future career in architecture, is the grasp of the essential nature of scale as it relates to the human physique, and how that understanding shaped my architectural designs. This concept found expression years later in my book, Scale in Architecture (Van Nostrand Reinhold, 1985).

The ID program had only one faculty member, Prof. L. C. Smith, at that time. He told that it was a very old joke with him to be asked if he was related to the manufacturer of typewriters. His reply was, "No, Shotguns!" Both products, as well as several others, were made by a company of that name.

One student design assignment during the third year was a coffee grinder. One classmate designed one in the shape of two cones, joined at the small ends, standing vertically. He had made a full size plaster model of it in the class shop next door, and left it one day at the end of class on a worktable in the far corner of the room. A buddy and I came in the next morning, arriving early, and saw it across the room, looking at it from an almost horizontal viewpoint.

After pondering it for a few minutes, we decided to embellish it with a couple of cardboard hands, colored in lifelike fashion, sticking out of the top, writhing in agony, as if a person had been consumed by the device. We left and came back when everyone else had come in, enjoying the joke along with all present except the designer of the coffee grinder. Even Prof. Smith was amused.

I suppose all college experiences have some of the same kinds of capers in them, especially in the creative fields. All I know is that it was a time of creative exploration, and, in the beginning at least, it was what I needed. It was not all fun and games. We engaged in some truly intense and difficult exercises and assignments, and I learned many valuable lessons from them, general as well as practical.

During World War II many if not all colleges and universities were asked by the government, or maybe required if they were getting government money, to change from the semester to the quarter system. I believe that the rationale was that it made it possible to graduate men quicker so that they could join the military sooner. Auburn kept the quarter system until sometime in the 1990's, so it was all I ever experienced in my two terms at Auburn. To my way of thinking, there are advantages to quarters, especially for technical fields, but what do I know? I'll let others argue this out.

My Aunt Mary Quiggle lived in Auburn with her family at the time, and she had found a room for me and a roommate in a private house sort of removed from the campus. That was OK, I didn't mind walking.

This house was just across the railroad tracks which crossed town east to west slightly north of the business district. My room was right beside the tracks, not fifty feet away. The depot was about a block east of our house, and when a westbound freight train came through about 2AM every night, the steam engine stopped right outside our windows. It would sit there for several minutes, huffing and hissing, and when it started up again it would shudder and chug vigorously and shake the whole house, especially the two occupants of our room. After a few weeks we became used to it and it never woke us up any more.

During that fall quarter I was visited by two men from Theta Chi fraternity. One was Arnold Fagan, a football player. I had to admit I had never heard of him. Given the record of Auburn football at that time, that may have been a valid excuse. I can't remember who the other man was. I didn't think I could afford membership in a fraternity, but the idea intrigued me. I was also contacted by a couple of other fraternities, but nothing came of that. Theta Chi offered me to pledge me, and after some initial reluctance, I accepted. This gave me an alternative to the railroad track room, and at the beginning of the winter quarter I pledged and moved into the fraternity house.

Being a fraternity pledge involved a certain amount of hazing, but I never found it to be oppressive. All pledges had to have wooden paddles, which were used mostly to intimidate the pledges. We, the pledges, were supposed to get our paddles signed by all the members, and often as not when doing so, we were asked (or was it "commanded?") to bend over for a little physical hazing. One weekend I was ordered to hitchhike to Auburn's arch rival, the University of Alabama at Tuscaloosa, with my paddle, to the Theta Chi chapter there, spend the night, get the paddle signed by as many of the members there as possible, and hitchhike back, leaving as many insults as I could get away with. Jack Ibach, my roommate at the time, already had been initiated and was a full-fledged member, but he had never been to Tuscaloosa and he voluntarily went with me. We made it there and back OK. That was about the worst hazing I had to endure.

When I pledged the chapter was beginning a new building program. At the old house I slept in a sleeping porch, a large enclosed but poorly heated room with six bunks for pledges and others who preferred to stay there. Our new house was built during the rest of my freshman year and into the next. It was designed by Edward Marty, a Theta Chi alum who taught in the School of Architecture. Its design might be called modern or "International Style." It has twenty two-man rooms, public spaces, a dining room, and similar facilities. It sits nicely on its lot, with graceful layered transitions up the slight rise of the land. Recently, however, the culture of fraternities has changed. Now it seems the chapter wants only rooms for the chapter officers, and more room for social events and such. A new design has been developed to replace the older house, which seems a shame to me, but I am not there now.

Each fraternity had an annual formal dance weekend, in which the men would move out of the house and their dates would move in. Ours was held in February, if I remember correctly. The first one held in our then new house occurred when the house was barely finished, and the street in front was paved only to the edge of our property. Huffing and gasping, we had to carry our dates, in their ball gowns, across several yards of muddy street and unsodded yard, both in and out of the house for the ball, as they squealed and giggled. It was a mess!

I made many friends in the fraternity, and this in my opinion is the most beneficial aspect of my membership. I still keep in touch with a few of them, and value their friendship.

Even though I enjoyed my classes, especially in NROTC and ID, after a couple of years I was convinced that I was in the wrong place, not at Auburn, but in my career track. I did well in ID, and plugged in properly and vigorously in NROTC, but I had let my social life begin to overshadow my academics. The various fraternity activities and some campus political things seemed to become more important to me than classes.

On the first of the NROTC cruises I was on the heavy cruiser USS Albany. Other midshipmen from all over the country served on this and a dozen or so other ships of various sizes and types. The entire fleet sailed from Norfolk and went across the Atlantic to Denmark and Holland.

We had liberty at all these stops, and in Copenhagen I was enthralled. Touring Fredricksborg Castle I was in a gallery overlooking the Chapel when I happened to look down at the railing and saw carved into the wood, the date, 1680. Nancy and I visited Denmark in 2003, and toured Fredricksborg. We looked for the carved date, but never found it.

While in Copenhagen, another Midshipman and I took a train north to Helsignor, the legendary home of Hamlet, and the site of the impressive Kronborg Castle. There we saw a group of actors rehearsing a production of that play, to be staged in the castle courtyard. After touring the castle we found an amusement park where we met and spent the afternoon with a couple of very nice young ladies. They spoke English better than we did, having had their lessons from teachers from England. My buddy was from Mississippi and had a southern accent worse than mine, so communication became rather comical at times. The girls pronounced "can't" as "cahn't"; we tried to teach them to say it our southern way, "cain't." I doubt if we accomplished anything more than a few giggles.

At Rotterdam some of us took an overnight tour to Brussels and Antwerp, Belgium, visiting the site of Napoleon's defeat at Waterloo. I remember that at Waterloo it was a dark, gloomy, rainy day, and the monuments were dark and gloomy also. The highlight, if there was one, was an old black and white movie, in French, about the battle. On the other hand, Brussels and Antwerp were interesting and enjoyable, especially the architecture of the Antwerp Guild Houses, from the thirteenth and fourteenth centuries.

After that the flotilla sailed across the Atlantic, and ended at Guantanamo Bay, Cuba, where we spent three weeks or so going through gunfire practice and other drills.. There wasn't a whole lot to do at Guantanamo Bay. We couldn't go off base, so we didn't see anything of the real Cuba. It was not unlike hundreds of other military bases anywhere in the world. One day when we had liberty, for a lack of anything else to do, another midshipman and I hitched a ride with two Navy pilots who need air time to maintain their qualifications. We flew around Cuba and across the Caribbean to the tip of Haiti for four boring hours. After you have looked down and seen the countryside and ocean below once, the thrill wears off when that's all there is to see over and over. It was my first airplane ride.

My second cruise began with three weeks at the Naval Air Base at Corpus Christi, Texas, where we had aviation indoctrination. One week of this was spent at Kingsville Naval Air Station, where we were cautioned to always shake out our shoes in the morning before putting them on, to be sure we didn't share the shoe with a scorpion. The town of Corpus Christi organized a very nice dance for us, inviting local young ladies to join us. While dancing with one such damsel, trying to be suave and clever, I asked her how many oil wells her family had in their back yard. She replied that they weren't in the back yard; they were on their ranch. So much for that.

After that we were transported by train across the country to a Marine base at Little Creek, Virginia. Here we had another three weeks, receiving training in amphibious warfare. The culmination was supposed to be a large landing exercise similar to that at D-Day and other operations in WWII. It involved many ships and the entire midshipman contingent from all NROTC schools and the Naval Academy. We arose early and loaded up on the ships, with full Marine battle gear. We were supposed to climb down the sides of the ships on cargo nets to barges, called lighters, alongside, and then into landing craft for the actual beach landing. The operation had only been going on a few minutes with just a few boats loaded and headed toward the beach, when things were suddenly stopped. A midshipman had fallen between the ship and a lighter and was crushed. The whole operation was cancelled, and we were carried back to shore. Most of us didn't learn the reason or the details until we got back to base, much later. When we did, it was sobering.

Before leaving Auburn for that cruise, another midshipman, John Arnold, and I had arranged to add on a week's stint on a submarine. Both of us thought we might want to go into subs after graduation. It was a training cruise. We were the only midshipmen aboard, but there were also reserve officers there, and we were treated just like them. It was heady, and I loved the experience. If I had stayed in the Navy I likely would have gone into submarines. The highlight of this cruise was a time when the boat stopped out in the ocean for a swim call. A submarine controls up and down movement when submerged by a pair of horizontal fins at each end, that move much like the elevator on an airplane does. When the boat is on the surface these, called bow and aft planes, are folded up against the hull so they don't impede movement through the water. When swim call was sounded, the bow planes were lowered to stand horizontal right at the waterline, and we could use them as diving platforms. A sailor was stationed on the conning tower with a rifle, looking out for sharks or other predators. We had thirty or so minutes of carefree swimming when the lookout called out, "Shark!" and fired off a shot. We all made a mad scramble to get out of the water as fast as possible. I have always suspected that the Captain just decided that we had had enough, and used this method to get us back aboard.

I was more and more convinced that ID was not what I needed to be doing. By the spring quarter of my junior year I was just coasting academically. A few weeks before the end of the quarter my classroom NROTC instructor called me aside and told me I was failing his course, Navigation, and that the only way I could pass it would be to get an A on the final. That somehow got my attention, and I studied harder than I had in many months. I got a B+ on the final, and I failed. This had the result of eliminating me from the NROTC program, canceling my scholarship. There were no retakes. While I had never been an outstanding student, this was the only course I failed during this time at Auburn. That summer I worked as a lifeguard at Hatfield Lake, a sort of budget level amusement park just outside of Athens, owned by the family of my high school classmate, Bobby Raney. In the fall I went back to Auburn, with my folks paying for everything. I really felt bad about that because I knew that they had limited funds, and two more sons were coming along who would need college money, also.

During the previous spring quarter I had been elected President of the fraternity chapter, and in the fall I took office. However, I was still dissatisfied, and felt that I should not cost my folks any more money than necessary. In addition, I didn't have a car and had to sponge from my fraternity brothers for dates and any other kind of transport. I did not return to Auburn for the spring quarter.

I re-enrolled in the summer, but quickly found that staying out of college that one quarter caused me to lose my draft deferment. The Draft Board began breathing down my neck. The quarter that I was not in college I worked in a grocery store in Athens, and during that time I applied for the Air Force pilot training program. I was sent to an air base in Georgia and went through a battery of tests and such, and was accepted. However, I was still hopeful that I could stay in college so I turned it down. That proved to be a forlorn hope. Uncle Sam was standing close by, with a uniform at the ready.

8.

CARS

"My car seems to be having transmission trouble," said Tom shiftlessly.

*O*ne of the great frustrations for me during college, except for one period I'll explain later, was that I didn't have a car.
All who know me reasonably well know that I am slightly fanatic about cars. This manifested itself at a fairly early age, around four, I believe. For my fourth birthday I was given a pedal car that to my mind looked just like the 1935 Ford Daddy owned at the time. I was more proud of that car than any other toy from that age; at least I remember it better. It broke my heart when Daddy accidentally backed his car into mine and bent the left front fender slightly. I am sure it was the left fender because I have a photograph of it, with me in the driver's seat, of course.

I yearned for the time when I could drive. Perhaps I was no different from any other boy in that way, but it became almost an obsession with me. One day I was with Mama when she was running some errands. She stopped at a house, I don't remember why or who it was she stopped to see. I was about nine years old. She was usually very careful about such things but for some reason she left the keys in the car, and left me there as well. She stayed longer that I expected, and I got restless. I slid over to the driver's seat. Of course

I knew how to turn the key on and push the starter (they were two separate things in those days), so I thought I'd try it. I had not yet learned that you also had to put the clutch in, and off I went, running the car into a conveniently nearby ditch. It didn't do any harm to the car, although it had to be towed out of the ditch. The harm was to my ego; I was mortified, and I prayed that none of my friends found out what had happened. I don't believe they did. This was in our 1941 Ford when it was fairly new.

In addition to drawing war machines during that time, I liked to draw cars, fanciful projections of how new cars would look after the War. This was inspired in part by the same sort of looking ahead done by the design departments of the automobile manufacturers, and reported in magazines. One focused effort, I suppose to prime future customers for what might be to come, was by General Motors. This was a program for young people to submit models of cars they had designed to be judged by the GM design staff. The prizes were scholarships to study design. I don't remember the name of the program, but I entered two years. My efforts were pretty bad, but I enjoyed doing it and the experience probably was driven by and had an impact on my interest in drawing and design. It was another avenue of expression for the creative urge that has always bedeviled me.

Before the War Daddy usually kept a car only about two years, and he always bought new cars. He put so much wear and tear on them, not to mention mileage, in his work that they must have worn out that quickly. Cars just didn't last as long then as they do today, for anybody. However, when the War came along, and new cars weren't available, he had to keep that old faithful 1941 Ford until the War was over, and then some. He didn't replace it until about 1949 with a Nash. In addition to not being a Ford, it was the first and only non-new car he purchased since marrying Mama, at least as far as I knew. It must have been a demo. As a young man, before marrying, he and a partner bought a used Model T, and had an accident driving it off the lot. I believe it was totaled. He suffered a slight injury to his right arm, and it was never quite right after that. He had somewhat limited movement in it, but he never let it bother him or keep him from doing whatever he wanted to do. Except for the Nash, he always bought new cars.

The Nash was the car I had use of my senior year and the next summer, and I was not particularly proud to be seen in it. The Ford was to my mind a more "gutsy" car, even if it was a little banged up. The family's next car was a bright red 1952 Ford, and except for the Nash and the Model T, the first non eight-cylinder car Daddy owned. All others had been V-8's. The 1952 was a stick shift model, as all his other cars had been, but it had a relatively new feature, overdrive, and was rather peppy. I was away at college by this time, but my brother, Johnny, had learned to drive. I don't remember if he had his license or not; we were rather casual about that sort of thing then. Anyhow, he wanted to show off the power that car had to some of his friends, and piled six or seven of them into it with him, revved up the engine and popped the clutch. To his surprise and chagrin, and the raucous amusement of his friends, the car didn't go anywhere. He had broken the ring gear in the rear end! After it was repaired, it served well for about three more years.

The last car Daddy owned was a 1955 Ford. Nancy and I took it on our honeymoon. After he died in 1959 Mama had several cars, none of which were Fords. I don't know if that means anything, but it seems a little significant in retrospect.

During my freshman year at Auburn I got into automobile ownership for the first time. I was led astray by a friend and fraternity brother, Ed Cornely. Ed lived in a sort of cottage in a cluster of the same built by a hotel in back of their property, located half a block from the famous Toomer's Corner. In the next door cottage lived an older student, a WWII veteran, I believe. This fellow had two Model A Fords. Ed decided he wanted a car, and one of these was available, but he couldn't afford it all by himself, so he recruited a partner, me. I couldn't afford it any more that he could, but the investment was only $25.00 each, and we scraped up the money and bought it. "It" was a 1928 roadster, with rumble seat, only the seat was missing. Some other parts were missing as well, such as a top, and a floorboard without holes. I found myself fascinated watching the roadway race by, looking down at the floor of the car. It also had little or no brakes. We learned to stop by down shifting and shoving it into reverse at the last moment. One of the brake shoes had worn completely through and had separated from the flange attached to the hub. It was simply a loose steel ring and made a wonderful sort of singing noise as we drove around till we got around to taking the wheel off and removing the offending brake drum.

We couldn't afford a license plate so Ed came up with a creative way to get around that little problem. In those days Alabama issued two plates, one for the front and another for the rear. Our friendly seller let us take the plate from the front of his other Model A, and put it on the rear of our car. This worked for a while, but one Sunday, when I returned from a trip home, Ed met me and told me that I owed him $15.00. He carelessly parked next to the other Model A, and a kindly Policeman noticed that the two plates were identical, and that was that. Ed had had to buy a plate and I had to come up with my share.

Another time when I returned from Athens, Ed handed me a small sum of money. When I asked what it was for he told me a wild tale that was hard to believe. I tended to believe it, though, because Ed Cornely was so tight that he would never just hand out money as a joke. He and some other of the good brothers had convened at a beer joint the previous Saturday night, and left our Model A parked outside. Some other friends had arrived in a different car. While inside a rather inebriated man none of them knew walked in and asked who owned the Model A out front. Ed admitted that he did, and after some discussion he sold the car to this gentleman for some exorbitant sum. So, Ed and at least some of the others left and went back into town in the other car. When he got to the fraternity house, he talked a fellow who hadn't been there to go out there and try to buy the car back. This proved to be a successful ploy, and he bought the car back for about half of the purchaser's cost, and the buyer hadn't even been out of the joint to look at it. Ed, our purchaser-agent, and I split the profit.

To get money to buy gas we sometimes drove around campus and elsewhere and picked up discarded cold drink bottles. In those years you could turn them in to the bottler for two cents each, and gas was only about thirty cents a gallon. One day we happened on a farm house with piles of old tires in the side yard. We knew our tires were on their last legs so to speak, so we stopped to see what kind of trade we could come up with. For two dollars Ed bought I believe eight tires that looked reasonably sound. The next day he took them to a recapping shop and made a deal whereby they traded him two recapped tires in exchange for all of the tires he brought in. Ed had a way of scrounging up things, among those replacements for the missing rumble seat.

One fine spring day several of us from the fraternity piled into the car and drove out to nearby Chewacla State Park. On the way back we ran out of gas. Even though I was co-owner of the car (I don't believe Ed was with us), being the only a Pledge along I was elected to go get gas. The part of the road we were on was long and straight but had slight hills. I had walked perhaps a mile and was just out of sight of the car when here it came, chugging along. Ed had found a kerosene lantern somewhere and stashed it in the car. I didn't even know it was there. The guys had poured the quart or so of kerosene from the lantern into the car, and it ran! Those Model A's were remarkable cars; they would run on just about any fuel, and, as we soon found out, on less than all four cylinders. One evening the next-door Model A owner we had bought ours from had lent his car to two other students to drive to an important function of some sort. Before leaving they had lubricated themselves up with substantial amounts of alcohol and were feeling fine. As a joke, Ed went over and pulled the spark plug wires off of two plugs. After a while the two fellows came out and got in the car and drove off. It maybe was a little noisier and ran rougher than usual, but they didn't even notice.

At the end of the Spring Quarter we had to make a decision about ownership. Ed and I were going our separate ways until the next fall. I don't remember if we flipped a coin or did it some other way. In whatever way, I lost and had to buy Ed out, for his original $25.00 investment. The car did not last too long after that and passed out of our hands, in rather poor shape, I'm afraid. The body of the car was so worn and weak that when we went around a curve it would rack and lean over, and it got worse as time went on. During that summer I had it at home in Athens and decided to improve things.

Even though I had always wanted a convertible, it simply had no top, convertible or otherwise. In a local junkyard I found a Model A coupe with a reasonably sound body, but a bad motor. I made a deal with the owner of the yard to buy his car for twenty dollars plus the body from my car. I towed the coupe to our house and parked the two cars side by side. After removing all the bolts and such from both cars, I persuaded some of my friends to come over and help me lift the bodies off the cars and swap them. I then bolted everything back in place and towed the now roadster back to the lot. When Fall Quarter began I didn't take the car back to college immediately, but waited until Spring Quarter. What I failed to do was to either drain the radiator or put in antifreeze for the winter, and it froze, cracking the block. I didn't realize this until driving back to Auburn I had to stop frequently and add water. When I got to Auburn I was unable to drive it much and it was an embarrassment. Soon a fraternity brother offered to buy it, and I agreed, for the princely sum of $15.00. So much for that automotive episode.

My next venture into automobile ownership was while I was in the Air Force. I had completed Basic Training and had been assigned to a Tech School on Kelly AFB, just down the road from Lackland AFB, where Basic Training was conducted. After completing the Tech School course I was asked to teach there. It looked like I would be staying there in San Antonio for a while, so I decided to get some "wheels." Through a friend I was led to a used car lot and was persuaded to buy a 1937 twelve cylinder Cadillac. It wasn't in really bad shape; it was just a lot of car and used gas and other consumables at exorbitant rates. After a few weeks I got a little more sensible and went back to the lot and traded it for a 1947 Chevrolet Coupe. This was a nice car and I enjoyed it until I was told that I would be shipped overseas and sold it back to the same dealer.

My overseas time was spent in Tripoli, Libya, not the kind of place one might expect to find a lot of options of cars to buy. I didn't really need one, so I did without for several months. I really was tempted, though, one time. I don't remember how contact was made with this fellow. A Libyan, he tried to sell me a brand new Morgan sports car. I drove it and fell in love with it. The price was only $1,200, but that was about $1,000 more than I could afford, so I reluctantly passed on it. Ever since then I have had a dream of one day owning a Morgan, but I probably never will. The only car I had in Tripoli was really Nancy's. As a serviceman I could buy a car in Tripoli without paying a huge customs fee, provided it was bought within the first year of my time there. That had lapsed when Nancy joined me in Tripoli after we were married. We bought a car from a friend who was being transferred to Crete, and to get around the customs had it registered in Nancy's name. She turned twenty-one about that time and I claimed that I had given her a car for her birthday. It was a 1951 Studebaker, one of the Raymond Lowey-designed bullet-nosed models. This was in 1957, and the car had been "rode hard and put away wet," but we hadn't paid a lot for it. In just a few months we found that we would be going back to the States early and had to get rid of the car. We made a deal to sell it to a German civilian. He paid us I believe $75.00 down and let us drive it until we left. On the day before we were to leave it just quit running. We turned it over to the buyer and agreed that he could have it for what he had already paid us.

On our way home we landed from our troop ship in Brooklyn, and being very naïve, we bought a car from a dealer there who marketed to returning servicemen. It was a 1951 Nash Rambler. On our drive home it broke down in New Jersey, and we spent three days having a crack in the block welded back together. We managed to get on home to Athens, and then drove it on to San Antonio when my leave was over. We kept it until I was discharged and we took it back to Athens. We traded it for a 1952 Plymouth when I went back to Auburn in 1959.

Since then we have owned many cars, of various makes. Several of them have been mostly for one or more of our children. One of the more memorable was a Post Office Jeep, bought originally for our son, Steve. It had the steering wheel on the right side so the mailman could reach the mailboxes easier. When he had gone on to more "advanced" vehicles, it went to his sister, Karen. Our street had no sidewalks, just shallow ditches. On the first day Karen drove it to school, our other daughter, Amy, was watching out of her bedroom window, and suddenly shouted, "Dad! Karen just wrecked the Jeep!" I jumped up out of bed (Karen's school started at some unholy hour, and I was still in bed). I ran out in my pajamas and bare feet and out to the street. Karen had turned into the street too sharply, and the Jeep had just sort of laid over into the ditch. With her driving, and I pushing, we got it out and her on her way again.

On Christmas 2001 Nancy gave me a "Richard Petty Driving Experience." There are several NASCAR tracks around the country where I could have gone to have this "experience," but we chose Nazareth, Pennsylvania because it is only about an hour from my brother Allen's home in central New Jersey. My drive came in May of 2002, and I enjoyed it immensely. I didn't set any speed records, I just gritted my teeth and took the allotted eight laps as fast as I felt like.

There were several other cars in the Orr family history, most unremarkable. I finally got my sports car, though, in 1995. It was not a Morgan, unfortunately. It was a 1967 Sunbeam Alpine, a dream to drive, but not in the best of shape. You couldn't find parts for it and it was in the shop about as much as it was on the road. In 2000 I got rid of it and replaced it with a 1992 Mazda Miata, replaced in 2005 by a 1999 Miata, which I drive every day. It is my everyday car, and I love it.

In my advanced age I have become convinced that those who design cars, or perhaps those who decide what features cars must have, may have gone too far. I believe that cars have become burdened with a lot of computerized bells and whistles we don't really need. Let me cite some examples. These unnecessary goodies just allow more and more things to go bad and need repairing, often at inconvenient times, always costing money we often don't have. You cannot find a car now less than about thirty years old without power windows. The first car we owned with them was a 1984 Nissan Maxima, not bought new, of course. The power window operators went out one by one until only the one by the driver worked. We finally decided that we had to get them fixed, to the tune of several hundred dollars. Window cranks always seemed to work just fine for me.

For many years I swore that I would never have a car with disappearing headlights. I had seen too many with one light popped up and the other still down, making the car look like a drunken bullfrog.

The first Miata, had them, and never failed. However, I'll be amazed if they don't any day now. Amy now has the 1992 Miata.

The last sedan we owned was a 1992 Taurus, bought used with about twenty thousand miles on it. I didn't especially want the twelve-way power seats, but the car came with them. Not long after we got this car I realized that the seat controls were only partially operable. Everything seemed to work except the reverse movement button. The seat would move forward, but not back. It was in a position that I could live with, and I knew that someday I ought to have it fixed, but I was in no hurry. One day Nancy and I took it to a carwash. When it was delivered back to us, the seat had been moved up so far toward the front that I literally could not get in the space between the seat and the steering wheel. I could not get in the car to drive it. I suppose that the cleaners had moved it forward in order to vacuum the floor in the back. Nancy, being the slimmer of the two of us, squeezed in and was able to drive it home. By jiggling the controls around and cursing and twisting my mouth around in strange ways, I was able to move the seat back just enough to give me room to get in and drive the car to the shop, and have the dratted thing repaired, again, to the tune of more dollars that I care to recollect.

Radios are another example. I like the old-time radios where you could turn a dial and find your station. No more! You have to find the station by punching buttons multiple times, sometimes overrunning the spot and backing up, and then locking it in. I like to control the volume by turning a dial, not tapping a button. Some of these radios, like many other devices we have become almost slaves to, require us to have an Owner's Manual handy in order to operate what could be a rather simple device, with simple purposes. Most car radios have multiple features that I don't understand and will never use. Why do we need all this for heaven's sake? We got along quite well without them for a long time, didn't we? I wonder why anyone needs a high-powered or super hi-fi radio in a car anyhow. To have a car in which all the road noise and wind noise has been acoustically screened out would cost more that most of our houses. Yet we are enticed to spend hundreds or in some cases thousands of dollars on these sound systems, equipment that we will never be able to hear at it's projected quality level, because the car itself makes too much noise unless it is standing still. That strikes me as pretty stupid.

I have some advice for anyone who may one day own a car.

1. Never buy a new car; they depreciate too fast. A good used car, suiting your needs, will always be available to anyone who takes the time to look for it.

2. If at all possible, do not finance a car. Pay cash. It may be your own cash or your parents' or your in-laws', but just don't pay the bank or a finance company to own a car.

3. As soon as possible, after getting out from under a lien if you are unable to do number 2., above, cancel all insurance except liability. If, ideally, you can pay cash for it, don't buy any insurance other than liability. This is called "Self-insuring." This is what I have done for many years, and it has paid off many times over. It will do so for you if you are a careful driver.

4. Don't think of your car as anything other than an appliance, something to perform tasks for you that can be accomplished in no other way. Grow out of the Junior High School notion that the car you drive says anything essential about who you are. It is just a tool. Learn to live with that.

I don't drive a sports car because of the "Statement" it may make about who I am, but because I like the experience of driving it.

9.

UNCLE SAM

When the knight walked into the blacksmith's shop, the blacksmith said:

"Welcome! You've got mail!"

I stayed out of college the spring quarter of 1954, and re-enrolled for the summer session. Still trying to find a way to get an officer's commission, during that spring I applied to the Air Force for pilot training, took a test and passed, but turned it down to see if I could find a way to complete my college degree. In the middle of that summer quarter I received notice from the Limestone County Draft Board that I had been reclassified One A, and should expect to hear from the Army soon. Recognizing the handwriting on the wall, I left school and went home to Athens. One of the first things I did When I arrived home was to hitchhike to Nashville and call on the Navy recruiting office. I had been led to believe that the active duty time I spent in the two summers with the NROTC would count toward longevity with the Navy. That turned out to be false.

Next I went to the Air Force recruiting office in Decatur, Alabama and inquired about re-instating my acceptance in the pilot training program. No go there as well. So, I enlisted in the Air Force then and there.

What was in the back of my mind was that I might still find a way to get a commission as an officer.

During AF Basic Training at Lackland AFB in San Antonio, Texas I applied for the Officer Training School, or OCS, and was accepted, but by the time I had completed Basic TrainingI had concluded that I didn't want to stay in any kind of military service any longer than necessary, and I turned that down as well. That probably was a wise move. I would have made a terrible officer, no matter what the branch of service. I realized that I preferred to think for myself more that the military likes, and that I ultimately would end up in trouble.

After Basic I was sent from Lackland to Kelly AFB, almost next door in San Antonio, for specialist training in a field that was and I presume is still classified, so I won't say much about it. There were two levels to the course. The first carried a lower classification, "Confidential," and security checks were conducted on us during the time of this course. The second part involved more highly classified material. When I completed the first phase, although I had passed the security clearance, I was asked to skip the next phase and to teach in the first part of the curriculum. This went on for some little while until a policy was proclaimed that anyone teaching in this specialist area must have field experience, meaning an overseas assignment. Because I had been sort of dumped into this situation in an off-cycle, that is, not when a whole class has completed the course, my options for assignment were limited to two – Alaska and Libya. Not caring very much for cold weather, I chose Libya.

I boarded a troopship in the Brooklyn Navy Yard in October 1955, sailing for Tripoli, Libya, with stops in various Mediterranean ports. The ship had a route making a circuit of ports, dropping off and picking up troops, dependants, mail, supplies, etc. as needed.

When we first boarded in Brooklyn everyone was given a work assignment, at least the enlisted men were. I had just found my space and stashed my gear in this large compartment, where bunks were stacked five high, when someone from the ship's crew came through and asked if anyone could operate a 16mm film projector. Conventional wisdom in the military is never to volunteer. However, this sounded promising, and if anything, I enjoy a challenge. I remembered my old TBPC experience from high school, and spoke up and was told to come along. It turned out that my assignment would be to show movies every night to a small contingent of the ship's crew who served dinner to the officers. The room this took place in had a snack bar, which was open to me. It truly was a plush gig, nothing like the duty everyone else had. Unfortunately, someone decided that it was too plush an assignment for one mere airman, and about two-thirds through the trip I was taken off and given a typical cleanup detail for the rest of the time.

Our first stop was at Casablanca. We were given the option of getting off the ship there but to do so we had to sign up for a tour, which cost more than I thought I needed to spend, so I stayed on board. I did make a sketch from the ship, however, of a carriage waiting on the dock.

The next stop was at Livorno, Italy. I did get off there because it is very close to Pisa, and I wanted to see the tower. In those days you actually got to walk all the way to the top, standing on the open roof with just a flimsy metal rail between you and the ground below. After that we sailed on to Naples, where I didn't get off the ship, but from the deck I did draw a sketch of the dockside.

Tripoli was our next, and for many of us, our last stop, and by that time we had been on board nine days.

One of my friends was assigned to the ship's bakery. When we left Brooklyn we wore khakis and donned dungarees for the passage. When we got to Tripoli, we had to put on dress blues, and my friend had gained so much weight from his access to the bakery goodies that he couldn't get into his uniform. He had to get special permission to sneak off, and was not allowed to be seen with the rest of us.

In Tripoli I was reunited with several of my former classmates from the tech school at Kelly. They had about five months seniority in Tripoli on me, but they quickly clued me in to the peculiarities of the base and the work. We lived in three-story dorms, with two-man rooms, and central toilet and shower facilities on each floor. On the first floor there was a day room with a television and a few lounge-type seats. The television received only programs broadcast by the base station. Programming consisted mainly of shows from the US, about six months late. Each room had a lavatory, backed up to the one in the next room, and because the rooms were identical on each floor, the lavatories were stacked as well. That means that there were six lavatories served by one sewer line and one vent pipe. We also had access to the roof for sun bathing, and some creative people discovered that the vent pipes for the lavatories, coming out on the roof, were just the right size to allow a beer can to be dropped down them, clogging the drain for six lavatories, causing an overflow on the first floor when put in use. Such fun!

The roof was also used for other things. One fellow was a model airplane builder. He had built a large gas-powered model plane, and had ordered an engine from the States for it. The engine didn't come and didn't come. After several months of frustration, he tied a rock on the engine compartment, stood on the roof, set the plane on fire, and sailed it off. It soared high and far, and went down in glorious flames.

During our free time we were usually allowed to go into Tripoli, to have a meal and just look around. There were some interesting sights to see. The old city had, and still has I suppose, fragments of Roman structures within a massive castle complex, and a history as one of the centers of the Barbary Pirate era. In fact, the phrase "The Halls of Tripoli" from the Marine's Hymn comes from what may have been the crucial battle in that campaign in which the US Navy and Marines crushed the Pirates. There was a mast still mounted on the castle parapet salvaged from a US ship that was scuttled in the harbor to bottle in the Pirate fleet.

Libya was an Italian colony from 1911 till WWII, and at the time I was there Italian was the primary European culture and non-Arabic language in Tripoli. There was a large and attractive cathedral, plus many public buildings in what might be called "Mussolini Modern" style. The central part of the city had a distinctly European feel. There were arcades and colonnaded street fronts and similar urban features. It has been over forty years since I was there and I don't know what may have been changed during that time. I hope very little. It was a charming place. In addition to the Italian part, there were typical Arabic sectors, with souqs and markets and other local centers of activity.

The route from the base into town went through a little settlement called "Souq el Juma," translated, "Market of Friday," we were told. I never did understand this because Friday is the day of worship for Muslims. Anyhow, there was tannery located there and we could always tell when we approached it because of the smell. I don't recall any Americans ever stopping there.

One of my closer friends and I went into town together frequently. We had found a small family-owned Italian restaurant we liked. The family had a daughter, Carla, about six years old, and we sort of became her American uncles. We went there to eat fairly often. One day he and I were just strolling around town and happened on a local street urchin with a basket full of baby rabbits. On a lark we bought one, having no idea what we would do with it. Later that day we went to the restaurant and gave the rabbit to Carla and immediately forgot about it. Some weeks later we returned to the restaurant and the family brought out the rabbit, which had grown to rabbit adulthood, and offered to butcher it and serve it to us! Somehow that is what they thought we had in mind. Our Italian language skills were very limited and we had no end of difficulty trying to explain that we had meant as a pet for Carla. I'm not sure they ever understood, but we didn't dine on him.

Another local attraction is the proximity of two rather extensive and largely intact Roman cities, Leptis Magna to the east and Sabratha to the west of Tripoli. My friends and I visited them more than once. The most memorable of these visits was to Leptis Magna during the filming of a movie, <u>The Legend of the Lost</u>, starring John Wayne, Sophia Loren and Rosanno Brazzi. Took lots of pictures, mostly of Loren, of course. Later, when we had been transferred back to San Antonio, this film came to the theaters there. Both my pal from Tripoli and I were married by then, and we took our wives to see it. It is a rather lousy film, one of Wayne's worst, but we enjoyed seeing it just the same. I have since seen it again on television, and the film hasn't gotten any better, but Sophia still looks great.

We also took drives into the interior of Libya, though not very far. The coastal area is rather fertile, separated from the desert by a low range of mountains. A drive into the mountains about as far as we cared to go took us to the town of Garian, where there was an abandoned prison camp for British prisoners of the Italians in the early days of the African campaign of WWII. The Brits had decorated the walls with large and somewhat risqué murals, which is what we all went to see. This site was known as "The Lady of Garian."

There is one other incident from this period, one I witnessed but did not participate in. Like all large and active seaports, Tripoli had its supply of places of questionable entertainment, such as a casino in the Ouadan Hotel, the largest and likely best in town, and brothels. The casino was all right for GI's to visit, but the brothels strictly were not. That didn't stop some from trying to get in.

The Libyan government wanted only foreigners, primarily seamen from merchant ships, to have access to such places. The way this was controlled was that a pre-printed permission slip was issued to the seaman, validated by having a rubber stamp of the ship's name on it. An enterprising Airman, an AP (Air Policeman), found a way to use our office facilities to print duplicates of these slips, and stamped them with the official "Confidential" stamp. It was said that he sold them for ten dollars each.

I don't know how long or well this worked. I only heard of it after he was caught. I thought he would be thrown in jail for life and given a dishonorable discharge. He was docked some pay and reduced one rank, and was on the job at his post at the gate the next day, shy one stripe, sadder but wiser, I trust.

Many Airmen in Tripoli went to Europe when they took leave. I didn't; I was saving my leave and money to get married, and I needed it. Nancy and I were married on April 13, 1957 while I was home on leave from Tripoli. I returned to Wheelus AFB after a six week leave, and Nancy joined me there a little later for the rest of my overseas tour.

However, we returned back to the States earlier than we expected. I'll explain how that came about in the next chapter.

Reporting back in at Kelly AFB in San Antonio in early December, 1957, put me in much the same environment that I had left two years before. It was seven months earlier than originally expected. There I was assigned to my old unit, and several Tripoli veterans were there. I did not teach as I had before leaving, but I did the same sort of work I had done in Tripoli. Much of it had to do with writing reports, and my supervisors complimented me on the quality of my efforts. This no doubt encouraged me to think that maybe writing would be a useful skill in my later life, no matter what that might be. The big difference from my earlier stint there was that I lived off base and was married, as were some of my long-term friends.

The Air Force had a policy of promoting enlisted men in groups of those with similar specialties and time in grade. All my contemporaries and I were Airmen First, or three-stripers. The time came in early 1958 to promote us all to Staff Sergeant. However, the AF was going through a "Reduction-in-Force," or RIF, at the time, and to facilitate this we were offered the option of taking the promotion and staying for the remainder of our enlistments, or staying at our present grades and getting out three months early. Having decided many moons before that I did not want a career in the military, I was not tempted to take the promotion. In addition, by that time we knew that Nancy was pregnant. When the time for her delivery came Nancy would be too far along in her pregnancy to travel safely back to Alabama. To have the AF cover childbirth expenses I would have to re-enlist for another two years minimum, So, I turned the promotion down and was discharged in April 1958, rather than July, my original discharge date.

I was informed that I was still in the AF Reserve for four more years, but it was my choice as to whether my reserve service would be active or inactive. I chose inactive.

10.

NANCY

"Many waters cannot quench love,
Neither can floods drown it."
Song of Solomon 8:7 (KJV)

I have mentioned my wife and love, Nancy, several times and in various places in earlier chapters. This is how we came together.

During a 30-day leave from the Air Force before reporting for transportation to Libya, I went home to Athens. I was sort of lost; most of my friends were off in college or married and settled down, many in other places, or in a few cases in military service. That fateful truncated summer quarter at Auburn in 1954 Bob Gentry from Athens, whom I had known both in high school and at Auburn, and I roomed in the same off-campus house. I recall one evening several of us were engaged in what we would have called a bull session, and as was frequently the case, the subject of feminine beauty came up.

One of the participants, a smart aleck (Yankee, probably) said something derogatory about Southern women. I spoke up and defended them, citing that Bob Gentry, sitting right there, had a sister who was one of the most beautiful girls anyone could find anywhere.

The first time I remember seeing Nancy Gentry was at a birthday party my brother Johnny had at our house. Nancy was a guest. I was around sixteen, and she about twelve. My recollection was that I thought she was a doll, if a little young for me.

I remembered those events when I got to Athens on leave and called her for a date. For some strange reason she accepted. She must have had a weak moment. We sort of kept it up after that, and in a manner of speaking have never stopped.

Nancy has that classic facial bone structure thought to be so desirable in beautiful women. She is reasonably tall, an impression enhanced by her poised and erect carriage. Just as my mother beat good grammar into me, Nancy's mother drilled into her good posture, and provided extracurricular activities to help her become a polished young lady. Nancy had ballet and elocution lessons during her growing up years. The result is that she carries herself to this day with charm and elegance. Recently I introduced her to a friend, who described Nancy as "Regal." To me she is simply "Perfect."

The Biblical quote above takes meaning when the next phase of our relationship is revealed. After Nancy and I had a total of ten dates during my brief leave, I left for my overseas assignment. I had arranged to arrive in New York a few days early to take in a few of the sights. I had never been there and there were several things I thought I ought to see when I had the opportunity. I took a room at the 54th Street YMCA and struck out to see the great city. One important stop was the Museum of Modern Art. That and Central Park are about the only sites I actually recall visiting, except for standing in line for a couple of hours trying to get into the Tonight Show, still hosted by Steve Allen then. I didn't get in. When it became time to report, I went over to the Brooklyn Navy Yard where I would catch a troop ship bound for several ports in the Mediterranean.

My tour was for eighteen months, and Nancy and I wrote to each other practically every day. Actually she probably did that more consistently than I. During that separation by "Many waters" I sent her my fraternity pin, which she accepted, and sometime later I sent her an engagement ring.

She accepted that, too.

She still has all my letters to her. I got rid of hers to me because when I came back to the States to get married I had no assurance that my gear would not be disturbed, and I knew that if some of the people in my unit found them they would not hesitate to expose us both to ridicule and embarrassment.

Nancy had been in college at Birmingham Southern College up until the time we decided to marry. She thought she could contribute more to the marriage if she developed some more marketable skills. So, she left college and enrolled in a business school, honing her typing and other clerical abilities.

After my initial tour at Wheelus Air Force Base in Tripoli, Libya, I still had another year and a half on my four-year enlistment, so I chose to spend them in Tripoli, which I had come to enjoy. Also, being there would give Nancy and me the opportunity to go to Europe on leave inexpensively. In addition, Nancy wanted to have the same overseas experience, so we had decided that after the wedding we would return to Tripoli.

When I arrived at home Nancy and my folks accosted me for having a "Yankee" accent! Naturally, I was not aware that I did, though I understood why. I had been among folks from all over the country for many months, and in constant contact with a roommate from Boston.

The wedding was set for ten days after I arrived. I had no idea of the preparations and protocol involved in a proper Alabama wedding. I was in a daze, and mostly just stood around and jumped when anyone spoke to me or informed me of my duties. I was so naïve and uninformed that I didn't realize that it was my responsibility to see to the marriage license. It dawned on Nancy on the morning of the wedding that we needed to take care of this little detail. Because it was Saturday, it took the intervention of Mama, who in years past had worked for the county Tax Assessor, to get the required office opened, so we could be "legal."

Despite the fact that the bride and groom saw each other on the wedding day before the ceremony, all went well, and it has "stuck." Johnny was my best man, and Allen and Nancy's brother Bob represented the family as groomsmen, along with two high school friends.

Another illustration of my naiveté about the mores of weddings is that I didn't have any definite plans for the honeymoon other than that we would leave Athens as fast as possible and just find our way on the fly. Jimmy Sibley, a high school classmate, was one of my groomsmen. His folks picked us up at the church and spirited us away to their house, where I had stashed our car. We drove south and made our way to Florida, with a couple of stops along the way. After looking around a day or so there, we turned back north and spent a night on St. Simons Island, Georgia. By that time I was out of money, and I wired Daddy to send us some, which of course, he did. We made it back to Athens without any more difficulty. Looking back, I find it somewhat amazing that Nancy has really stuck with me after that unplanned, care-free beginning. Blessedly, she has.

When that leave was up I had to go back to Tripoli, but Nancy had to wait for a passport with her new name on it. Servicemen, at least then, did not have to have passports. It was about six weeks after I went back before she could come over. By today's standards communication methods available between countries separated by oceans were rather primitive in 1957. A transoceanic telephone call was a major undertaking, involving making an appointment perhaps days in advance. The sensible alternative was a cable, which I sent after stewing for many days and thinking of all sorts of dire catastrophes, the worst that Nancy could have somehow decided that she really didn't want to come to Tripoli after all. She never even had those thoughts and she finally arrived several weeks after I did, to my great relief.

Before leaving Tripoli for the wedding, I had made tentative arrangements to rent a small apartment on the top floor of a four story building off base that a friend and his family had recently moved into. The building was still under construction. They rented a ground floor unit, which was finished, but the upper floors were still being built when I left.

The construction was very interesting. The walls were built of laid up chalk-like blocks quarried out in the interior of the country. No conduit for electrical wires were installed. Rather, after the walls were in place the workmen simple chiseled out ruts in the blocks, laid the wire there, and then covered them over with plaster. Pipes for plumbing were installed the same way. Floors were constructed by spanning a space with small 4" diameter poles, about 8" apart, laying a woven palm leaf matt on the poles, and pouring concrete on top of that. Finished floors were marble tile, and walls were plastered. Nevertheless, the exterior and interior finished spaces looked very nice. I liked what I saw, it was conveniently located, and I was looking forward to living there.

I stayed on the base until Nancy arrived, and searched out my friend and asked him if the building was finished so I could make final plans to move in. "No," he said, "The building collapsed and we had to move out and find another place!"

That meant that I too had to find another place. I scrambled after that to find such a place I did, and it was a delight. It was a small duplex, located right across the street from the beach in a district of Tripoli known as Giorgimpopoli, as close to a honeymoon cottage as anyone could ask. Named, "Villa Maria," it was likely built the same was as the ill-fated apartment building, but it was only one story, and had been there many years, so we felt safe enough. It had a large combination living/dining room, kitchen, bedroom and a bathroom. We got hot water by building a fire in a little wood-burning water heater in the bathroom. If you wanted to take a bath, you had to build a fire and wait until enough hot water was produced.

The kitchen had a small stove using bottled gas, in containers similar to those used in backyard barbeque grills today. There was a miniscule refrigerator, and the water, while abundant, was not potable. Nancy had to wash vegetables in water mixed with Clorox. For drinks we relied on cold drinks and the like.

In addition to finding a place to live, I had arranged, before going home, to buy a car and some furniture from friends who were being transferred to Crete. I didn't have to take possession until I got back.

Included in the deal was the temporary care of their boxer, Kim, until arrangements could be made to ship him to Crete. This dragged on for some months, but we both enjoyed having him around. He was especially useful in discouraging beggars and the like from bothering us. Like most individual homes in Tripoli, our little "villa" had a head-high openwork masonry fence around the yard, and no one not invited would attempt to come in because of the presence of a large ferocious-looking, but actually harmless and loving, dog.

While we put up with the lack of much we would have considered necessary back home in the States, at Villa Maria we enjoyed the location, the very good weather, the gorgeous sunsets, and each other. It was a good time, in a good home, and it was fun.

My work for the Air Force involved rotating shifts. My group would work three days, eight AM to four PM, then skip a day and change to three days four to midnight, then change again to three days midnight to eight AM. Then we would have a three-day break before starting all over. It was dull, repetitious, and mentally sapping work, a crazy life, and not one I would recommend to anyone.

Complicating our life together, Nancy had a job as a clerk-typist with a Libyan-American government-funded outfit whose task was to help Libyan development, especially in water supply projects. Her schedule, though different, was as weird as mine. The result was that there were long periods that we didn't see each other with much regularity. One evening someone brought a mixed-breed pup into the building where I worked and asked if anyone would take her home for a pet. I thought that she would be a good companion for Nancy when I couldn't be there, so I took her. Sammy, for Samantha, was our first "child," and we doted on her. Knowing that Kim would be leaving at some point, we treasured Sammy for our own.

When I left for home before the wedding the AF had a policy of providing a housing supplement for all married men of whatever rank who had to live off base, mostly because there was limited base housing available. After I returned the policy changed to restrict the supplement to officers and career enlisted men. I was neither, so we did not qualify for this additional money. That made it very hard to live on what we made, even though both of us were working. I filed a formal request for a reversion to the old policy for me, justifying my claim on the basis that it was in place before I left, and I had made plans based on having the supplement when I returned with a "dependent," as wives and families were called. The policy was actually changed while Nancy was in the air flying to Tripoli, so we were blindsided, and left in strained circumstances. One other airman on the base was caught in the same situation, and filed a similar claim.

Figure 10-1: Nancy and Sammy, 1957

Surprisingly, the brass decided that indeed we had been caught in a bureaucratic squeeze. We were offered to option of returning to the States early, in fact immediately. We decided to do this, and in October boarded the USS Patch, an Army troop ship, sailing to New York. We were disappointed, but at ease about it.

Before leaving, though, we had to get rid of the gear, furniture, car, etc. we didn't plan to take with us. The fate of the car I have described earlier. Somehow we sold off or gave away the furniture and other stuff. Even then we packed a huge crate of stuff to be shipped home.

We gave Sammy to the friends who had helped me find our villa, and in whose home we spent the first night Nancy was in Tripoli. Unfortunately on board the Patch Nancy and I had separate quarters. I was in a large troop compartment similar to that I had going over, but slightly less crowded. Nancy was in a cabin with three other women. I didn't have a work assignment, and until we got to Italy could wear civilian clothes. That changed, probably because some higher ranked officers came aboard then. After that I had to wear a uniform.

We were on the remainder of the Mediterranean circuit taken by the troop ship on which I came over to Tripoli. At each stop we had roughly a full day for sightseeing. Athens came first. A fraternity brother from Auburn had been stationed at Wheelus and transferred to Athens before we left. He was in the Air Force Post Office, and when we learned we would be in Athens on that particular day, I wrote to him and asked if he could meet us at the ship. When we arrived we turned down the chance to take an escorted tour, hoping that he had gotten my letter and would meet us. He never came, so we were just standing on the dock wondering what to do when a taxi driver asked us if he could show us around. We negotiated a price of fifteen dollars for an all day tour, and it was one of the best bargains we have ever had. Not only was the cost about half that of the other tour, we had a personal tour guide who knew his stuff and had great pride in his city. He not only took us to all the major sites, the Acropolis, the National Museum, and the 1896 Olympic stadium among several other places; at lunch time he took us to a genuine neighborhood restaurant for a traditional Greek meal. It was a delightful day, one we'll always remember and treasure.

Just before leaving Tripoli I had bought a movie camera at the PX, and we used it extensively on this trip back to the States. I already had a still camera, but the movie camera was a novelty, and I was still infatuated with my beautiful wife, so many of the scenes I shot with it seem to have Nancy in them.

At the next stop, Smyrna, Turkey, it was almost dark when we arrived, but we got off the ship anyway. We had a tour of some of the antiquities at Ephesus, and a trip to a bazaar where I bought Nancy an antique-looking bracelet. Because it was so late and dark, I didn't take the cameras along. We next went to Istanbul where we had signed up for the escorted tour. We saw the Blue Mosque and the Topkapi Museum, but the highlight for me was the Hagia Sophia, as I have described earlier. Seeing it changed and indelibly established the direction of my life, although I took a number of detours and made several false starts along the way..

After leaving Istanbul we sailed through the Strait of Messina, between Italy and Sicily, and on to Naples. There we got off the ship very late at night and got on a bus for Rome. We had arranged to take a two-day escorted tour in Rome, and then take a train to meet the ship again at Livorno. Even though we arrived in Rome about four AM, we were checked into our hotel and bedded down until we started the day at seven.

We saw every major site that could be crammed into that limited time, including tossing coins over our shoulders into the Trevi Fountain, insuring that we would return to Rome. We saw, among other sights, the Forum, the Coliseum, and one that is especially fascinating to me, the Pantheon. Not only is this building intensely interesting in many ways that are appealing to an architect, it also is the result of the Roman's structural inventiveness. It is one of the most important buildings from the Roman era, and it was built of concrete, a material they developed and exploited, and which was lost to civilization for centuries. Laid up between the inner and outer faces of the magnificent dome at the Pantheon are rows and rows of hollow clay vase-like elements, following the curve of the dome. These provide not only form but also rigidity and reinforcing to the structure, and they reduce the weight, making it feasible to build, for it's time.

One other special thing was a trip to Castel Gandolfo, the Pope's summer residence. We had an informal audience, along with a couple of hundred others, standing in the courtyard when Pius XII came to the window and blessed the crowd. Almost everyone else was kneeling and shouting, "Viva Papa!" but Nancy and I just kept standing and I shot movie film. Not to be disrespectful, to us he was just another nice old gentleman.

We breezed through Casablanca, our next stop, doing the usual tourist stuff and visiting a Sultan's Palace. The last stop was at the Azores, where we had only a brief time ashore, and no sightseeing.

We had our first Christmas together back in San Antonio. We had found a tiny apartment, cobbled together and tacked onto the back of a garage. There was barely enough room to turn around. There was one gas heater for all three rooms. Even though the whole apartment was probably no more than 300 square feet in area, that one heater was inadequate. We bought a small electric heater to help ourselves, and the landlord complained about the electric bill.

The commode and shower were in a tiny room off our bedroom. It was so small you had to come out into the bedroom to dry off after a shower. The lavatory was in the bedroom, but we really didn't mind. We were happy and excited to have a home.

We had a miniscule Christmas tree and presents from our parents, but practically no money to buy each other anything. Shades of "The Gift of the Magi!" The stove was an ancient apartment-size gas range, impossible to properly toast bread on, so we decided to treat ourselves to a toaster for Christmas, our only gift from each to the other.

We went to Sears and found one, an old-style totally manual model with drop-down doors on each side. You had to watch carefully or the bread would burn. When one side of the bread is done, you open the doors and close them again, and the bread automatically flips over, toasting the other side. This is the only automatic feature of this device. I believe we paid about $2.50 for it. We took it home still in the box, and Nancy wrapped it up for Christmas. We looked forward to that day when we eagerly anticipated having toast and jelly, prepared on our new purchase.

On Christmas morning we unwrapped it and opened the box in anticipation, only to discover that the package did not contain an electric cord! Worse, the cord seemed to be sold separately. Christmas being a holiday, Sears was not open so we could not go back and buy the cord that day. Later we did, and we used that toaster for some years. I don't know what happened to it, but I recently saw one just like it advertised in a catalog from The Vermont Country Store, for $52.95!

My discharge came through in April 1958, and we happily packed up our 1951 Nash Rambler and a trailer, and headed for Alabama.

One of the most endearing things about Nancy is the sense of adventure she shared with me from the beginning, and has never stopped doing so. Not every girl would get married and immediately leave to go live in a strange and foreign land. Ours is a partnership of equals. We simply enjoy this kind of life together, always willing to take up a new challenge, see new places and try new things. I cannot express how grateful I am that she has consented to join her zany husband in this wild ride of a life. To me, she is the most wonderful and beautiful woman in the world, and she grows more wonderful and beautiful every day.

Figure 10-2: Nancy, 2005

11.

FINDING FOCUS

"Knowledge and timber shouldn't be much used till they are seasoned."
                                    Oliver Wendell Holmes

We came home to Athens after leaving the Air Force, with all our possessions in a rental trailer in tow behind our little 1951 Nash Rambler, bought in Brooklyn when we landed. I had little trouble finding a job with Brown Engineering in Huntsville. Brown, since becoming Brown Teledyne, was a diversified government contractor, undertaking any number and variety of projects the government offered. I went to work there shortly after arriving back in Athens in April 1958.This was only a few months after Russia had launched Sputnik and America was in a mad scramble to catch up. Because Redstone Arsenal at Huntsville had become the center of American rocket research after WWII, much of the US effort in space technology fell to this location. Somewhat later NASA was organized and the facilities dedicated to the space program activities at Redstone were renamed the Marshall Space Fight Center.

While still in Tripoli I had applied for a position with the US Foreign Service. Before I left the Air Force in San Antonio I received notice that I could take an examination for this, which I did in Austin. Now, after becoming a civilian again, I was notified that I had passed the exam, and was invited to St. Louis for an interview. I knew that I would not be accepted immediately because I had not completed my undergraduate degree, but I thought it might be possible to get connected some way and get on track to be hired in the future as I worked toward my degree. I had always intended to go back to college, and what I majored in would be determined in part by what encouragement I received in this interview. What I was told at the interview was that, while I had done well on the written exam, my lack of a degree and the results of the face-to-face evaluation by the committee, led them to recommend against my application. It was an interesting experience, and I'm glad I went through it. It helped me to find my focus, increasingly narrowing it down to architecture as the right career path.

I worked at Brown for seventeen months during which our two sons were born, Mark on August 25, 1958 and Steve on September 14, 1959. My work was with a group of commercial artists whose primary task was to produce illustrations for technical manuals for rockets, space vehicles, miscellaneous weapons systems, and their components. Early on we undertook some very interesting projects outside our main focus, such as a space-themed mural for a bank. It was a time of learning some very helpful things about the technical side of producing commercial art. This became useful later when I needed to make some extra income. I had settled into a routine and got lazy and gained weight.

During my stay in Athens before returning to Auburn I was asked by Jerry McGivney, who had a house plan drafting service, to take over one project for him. I completed this, in what I believe was a satisfactory manner. In a small town like Athens everyone knows everybody else, and the owners of this house were close friends to Mama. If they had been dissatisfied I would have heard about it, and I never did. This opened the door for another possible revenue stream, which I was able to exploit from time to time. McGivney was to play an important part in my career many years later.

Just two weeks after Steve was born, in the fall of 1959, with God at the helm, I re-enrolled in Auburn, this time with architecture as my major. That first quarter Nancy and the boys stayed in Athens with her parents and I lived in a room in an off-campus house.

At Auburn I walked everywhere. About the only times I used the car were when I went home to Athens on weekends. I lost over twenty pounds in the first quarter, and probably was in better shape than in many months before.

Because of my earlier course work in Industrial Design, I was admitted as a sophomore in Architecture. I jumped right in, loving it. Here I was, on average, eight years older than my classmates, one of the very few married and even fewer with children, but that didn't seem to make any difference to anyone, student or faculty. Most of my courses were in the architecture curriculum, with a few electives, and required courses in math and physics, for example. Many of the more basic courses I had taken in my first "tour" at Auburn – in English, history, etc. – had transferred.

After Christmas Nancy and the boys came down to join me, and we moved into some rather primitive married student housing provided by the university. These units had been built in WWII, and were prefabricated. Even though they were old and shabby, they were reasonably roomy and comfortable. Our first apartment had two bedrooms and was located second from the end in a long row of similar units. The walls were made of four foot square panels of a sandwich of two layers of asbestos cement board with insulation between, about an inch and a half thick overall. These were fitted into a framing grid of wood 4X4's, routed to receive the wall panels. Acoustical insulation was not a strong quality. One day the wife in the unit on our right had an appointment to go somewhere with the wife in the unit on our left. She was running late and knocked on our wall, and yelled, asking Nancy to knock on the wall of the unit on the other side and tell that girl that she would be ready soon.

When it became available we moved into a three-bedroom unit, and were a little more comfortable. Being an architecture student requires somewhat more space to do things at home than in the studio. Interestingly, the new College of Architecture Building, built in the 1980s, was situated right where our apartments had been.

Although I was on the Korean GI Bill, and had that income, it was not enough. Nancy found a job as the Program Director at the Student Center. We employed a nice young lady to take care of the boys in our house. If daycare as we now know it was available, we didn't know about it, and probably couldn't have afforded if we had. In addition, I found freelance work producing artwork for the publications office of the Agricultural Extension Service, plus an occasional odd artwork job for others. The opening at the Extension Service came up because of Daddy's connections with that organization and the people there.

During my first time at Auburn the Dean of the School of Architecture and the Arts, as it was named, was a long-term professor named Frank Marion Orr. You can guess what kind of confusion that led to. Many of my classmates just assumed that I was his son, which was not a benefit, because Dean Orr was not universally liked. When I returned in 1959 there had been a wholesale turnover of faculty and administration. Dean, by that time just Professor, Orr was still around but on the faculty of the Building Science program, not architecture. There was a new Dean and all the architecture faculty was new as well. There was an excitement that was very real and energizing. Everyone, student and faculty alike, felt he or she was taking part of something very important and timely. Among the more memorable teachers were Robert Anderson, who taught my first design class, and Ralph Knowles, both of whom later moved on to teach at USC. Also Stan Thomason, who, when I decided to leave the architecture program for financial reasons, tried to talk me out of it, and even offered to lend me some money. I was touched. Knowles made a name for himself, first at Auburn and later at USC in the study of passive energy-conscious building design.

In a second-year class taught jointly by Knowles and Thomason we engaged in one of the most mind-expanding studies one could imagine. With a grant from a large manufacturer of corrugated cardboard, they led us through a long series of related and sequential exercises. First we examined the technical and structural qualities of cardboard, putting it through all sorts of tests and experiments to determine what were the construction possibilities of this rather mundane material. Through these activities we derived the modulus of elasticity and other technical indexes used in structural design with steel and other materials. We then designed and built small scale models, followed full size prototypes of modular units of a "building" to be later built as a whole. The prototypes were designed by small teams, and then the class and teachers jointly decided which design to build for the final phase. The design I worked on was not chosen, but the whole class went in together to build the one selected, as a "Museum" to the idea of cardboard as building material. It was erected on the ground in front of Biggin Hall, the architecture building. Unfortunately, it rained before it was finished and kind of washed things away, but it had been a roaring success as a learning experience.

In later classes and years our design assignments, called "problems" in architectural education jargon, became more complex and more specific. One was a multi-phase course in the third year, which began with the site planning of a new small housing development by small teams of students, and concluded with the design of the houses to be built in the development, designed individually by each student. Because I was the only married student in the class, I chose to design a "Bachelor" house; everyone else designed a typical three-bedroom family house. I thought that switch made it an even field. The faculty seemed to agree, although this turned out to be one of my earlier "Juried" design problems, and I received plenty of probing, but constructive, criticism. In this process a student is required to bring his design and present it to a jury of several faculty members and sometimes outside architects, none of whom except for the class instructor, has had anything to do with the problem. It can be a devastating experience, but it tends to, like the proverbial thought of hanging, "focus one's mind." There are still mixed views on the efficacy of this technique. I'll let others hash that argument out.

I thoroughly enjoyed my design classes, and at last I was making A's..

I made many friends in the architecture classes; one of the closest is Bruce Knodel, who went on to have a practice in Mobile. We were teamed together on several design projects, and often studied together. One night he came over to our apartment to study with me, leaving about midnight. A few minutes after he left there was a knock on the door. Bruce had returned, saying that his car had been stolen. I went out with him and looked around, but we found no sign of it. So, I took him to the police station and reported the theft, and then drove him home. Our building was on a rather steep slope, and at the end the street made a 180 degree reverse back up to the next row of apartments. At the bend of the street the hill continued on down slope, through some woods. The next morning as I walked through the woods to class, there was Bruce's car, lodged against a tree about fifty yards down in the woods. Apparently he had failed to set the brake properly, and it had started rolling downhill while he was in our house and continued on down until stopped by the tree. There didn't seem to be any damage and he came and retrieved it later that day.

Another area of study in the architecture curriculum was architectural history. Edward Marty, who had designed my fraternity house, taught this series of classes. I was perhaps a leg up on most of my fellow classmates because I had been in military service and had traveled more and had actually seen some of the more remote sites we studied. I did a paper on my impressions of the Hagia Sophia in Istanbul, which included a three-dimensional cutaway rendering of it (See Figure 1, in the Prologue), illustrating the structural intricacies of this magnificent building. Another feature of these courses was the requirement that we build a model of an approved historic building, usually in teams of students. Bruce Knodel and I, along with another student, built a model of Queen Hatsepsut's Temple in the Valley of the Kings in Egypt, which, with Nancy, I was able to visit years later. It fulfilled all my expectations and more. It is just dazzling, glowing in the relentless Egyptian sunlight, intimidating all who would dare to approach it. You can only come toward it from the prime axis, and in it's ascending ramp to the first level, and stair to the next, it overpowers you with the discipline to follow this path it imposes on you.

One of the real stars of classroom and studio in our architecture courses was another good friend from those days, Chris Risher. He now has a practice in Jackson, Mississippi, and has taught architecture at Mississippi State and as a visiting professor at Harvard. He and I studied together, and he was known to sometimes cadge a meal or maybe just a snack at our house.

Mama, who by this time was widowed and putting Allen through college on her own, helped us financially a little each month. Even with Nancy working and my irregular freelance work we weren't making it. By the beginning of Spring quarter 1961 I had concluded that we could not make our finances stretch out over the remaining two years remaining to complete my architecture degree, and felt oppressively guilty for taking Mama's limited money. It was time to do something. What I decided was to change my major back to Industrial Design and finish as quickly as possible. That took two more quarters, and I graduated in December 1961.

During those last two quarters I found a job as the Art Director of the public television station located at Auburn. Alabama has a statewide public television network, with at that time three production centers, one at Auburn, one in Birmingham and the third at the University of Alabama in Tuscaloosa. There not being then any NPR or other national public broadcasting network, each of the three was responsible for roughly one third of the programming hours. At Auburn we produced a wide variety of shows – sports, weather, horticulture, and music to name a few. I produced titles, credits and various illustrations for almost all of them, and designed and sometimes help build sets and props for a few of them.. I even ran a camera from time to time and appeared on-camera occasionally. One of those was as part of a small group singing Christmas carols. Another time, while a selection from Swan Lake was playing on the audio, I drew rather frantically, on a large board, abstract visual impressions of the music. One of the regular productions was a weekly cooking show, and the hostess, a home economics professor, brought in and cooked on-set something always very good. We all looked forward to this because after the show we got to eat what she had cooked. Another show was about woodworking, and while I was there the station received as a donation from one of the major tool manufacturers, an entire new shop of stationary and hand powered tools. The station was so poor, and resourceful, that we used the wood in the crates the tools came in to build sets and props.

There was no color; it was all black and white, but we did have videotape, a huge machine with tape that must have been 1" wide, on reels. One of the reasons we had the taping capability is that a WWII veteran from nearby Opelika, Alabama, had "liberated" the technology for video taping in Germany after the war, and had patented it in the US, and built a business on it. He was an Auburn alum and made it possible for the Auburn station to have that equipment. His name is Hubert Orr, and, sadly, is not kin to us as far as I know.

All of the experience of this period occurred in Alabama, using Alabama resources. Everything we experience shapes us. In Auburn it was joked that the reason the land-grant state agricultural college was located in Auburn is that the weather and climate is so varied there that it has to be the duplicate of that found in some region of the state at some time, and that it will acclimate the agricultural grads to any state location. In the summer it can be beastly hot. In the winter it rains a lot and is penetratingly cold. Especially during my first time in Auburn few if any buildings were air conditioned, and I remember in the warm months seeing people working over their drawing boards struggling to keep from dripping sweat on their work.

Nevertheless, Auburn is a wonderful place. It seems to get in the blood. I know of several of our friends in Nashville whose children have gone to Auburn, and they all have the same loving, and sometimes obnoxious, loyalty. In addition to Daddy, Allen and numerous cousins who attended Auburn, we sent our daughter Karen there. Another friend who had sent his daughter instead to the University of Alabama accused me of child abuse. Nancy's brother, Bob and his three sons all attended Auburn. It is not just the athletics, nor just the academics. It is not just an institute of higher learning. It is a mystique, a magical spirit that gets into your being and won't let go. Auburn, as it should be obvious to the reader, is one of the most important influences in my makeup. It is very special, and uniquely Alabama.

PART TWO

12.

ARCHITECTURE

One architect asked another, "If you won a million dollars in the lottery, what would you do?"

The other replied, "I'd keep on practicing until it ran out."

*E*ven though I identified architecture as early as the ninth grade as what I wanted to do, when the time came I sort of fell into it.

In an earlier chapter I told how I enrolled in architecture at Auburn after leaving the Air Force and working for several months, and then after two and a half years switching my major back to industrial design just so I could graduate sometime before the next millennium (slight exaggeration). I went looking for a job wherever a prospect turned up, mostly in industrial design or commercial art, which had been sort of a fallback revenue producer from time to time for several years. Trips to Atlanta, Savannah and Cleveland, Tennessee, didn't produce anything.

We came to Nashville in hopes of my getting hired as the Art Director at a new public television station being started, the same job I had had at the station at Auburn my last two quarters there. The manager of the Auburn station had been in Nashville on a year's leave of absence, helping to set up the new station, and he had given me an introduction to the management in Nashville. However, when I arrived, I was told that the need for that position was at least six months in the future. I decided to look for a job elsewhere. Looking through the phonebook, I saw two or three industrial design firms listed, and I began to call on them. The first two didn't have any openings. There really isn't a lot of call for this service in Nashville, and these firms didn't usually stay around very long. The third, I found out on the telephone, was really an architectural firm. They were listed as industrial designers in the phonebook because they designed industrial plants, not at all what my collegiate major was about. Here, I thought, was a different opportunity. Even though my degree was in a different, though related, field, I knew that my first love truly was architecture. They invited me to an interview, and I was hired. I reported for work at the firm of Edwin A. Keeble Associates on January 25, 1962.

I was really green. Having never worked in an architectural office, I didn't know a lot of the terms and procedures, and must have looked very inept to the seasoned workers I found myself among. Though not large by today's standards, Keeble's firm was among the largest in Nashville at the time. It was a "full-service" firm, having on staff engineering capabilities in structural, mechanical, plumbing, and electrical disciplines. Fortunately, the others there took me under their wings and mentored me into a halfway productive worker. Keeble himself took an interest in me and gave me things to do that tested and challenged me, and forced me to learn and grow. Even though I had just graduated from college a few months earlier, I was about eight years older than others in that same situation, so I must have exhibited a little maturity. Besides, I had a family to feed and was eager to get all I could from the experiences.

Within a year I was given a project to run, and was called a Project Manager. There were many more projects after that, of increasing importance and complexity. The title "Project Manager" is not defined the same way in all architectural firms. At Keeble's, being a Project Manager meant that one was responsible for the design, the coordination of engineering, the production of construction documents for the project, and for the site visits and other activities and responsibilities during construction. In many firms today these activities are separated and often performed by different individuals, or even different departments. Not so there. It was a marvelous experience; one I wouldn't take the world for, and one that today's architectural interns rarely will have the opportunity to experience.

Keeble knew early of my interest in church design, and gave me every opportunity he could to work on churches. Among my earliest projects was the renovation of the First United Methodist Church of Athens, Alabama, where Nancy and I had been married. Though his architectural degree was from the University of Pennsylvania, Keeble was also a Vanderbilt University grad, and so were some of the prominent members of this church, and that was how he was hired for this project. Nancy had grown up as a member of this church.

The project was a substantial alteration of the Sanctuary, changing the "business end" from the more conventional (for the time) arrangement of a central pulpit with the Choir arrayed across behind, into a split chancel, with the pulpit on one side and a lectern opposite. The pulpit has a canopy, or "Preacher Snuffer," hung above it. The Choir is divided in typical liturgical fashion, and a deep red dorsal cloth and large gold-colored cross hung in the center back wall, standing tall over the altar table below. All of this is a more liturgical arrangement than it had been, and more in keeping with the movement toward that stance that United Methodists were making at that time.

In addition, we introduced a new, rather bold color scheme for the Sanctuary, and included in the project some lesser remodeling in other areas of the church.

However, most of the churches I worked on at Keeble's and since, in my own practice, have been Baptist. The reasons for this include the fact that I am a Baptist and naturally have more contacts in that group, and also that there are just more Baptists in our part of the world than other denominations. Consequently, more of the churches being built are Baptist.

Figure 12-1: First United Methodist Church,
Athens, Alabama, Interior

Nashville is the home of the Sunday School Board of the Southern Baptist Convention, or BSSB for short. The name has recently been changed to LifeWay Christian Resources. For many years it has had a Department of Church Architecture. Originally, and until recently, this department has been a resource for churches and architects serving churches, offering guidance, standards, rules of thumb and other helps in order to promote better planning and design in church buildings. They hosted church architecture conferences every year or so, accompanied by a design awards program highly prized in the profession. Over the years I have participated in these conferences as a presenter, a juror of the awards program, and as an award winner on more than one occasion. Due to a change in focus by the LifeWay management the Church Architecture Department has evolved into a full service architectural office, competing with private firms like mine. I remain friends with the folks there, just as I am with my other competitors in the profession. In fact, as of this writing, there are three of my former employees working there, Kevin Goins, Regina Thompson, and Mike Robbins. I have jokingly accused the Director, Davis Byrd, a good friend, of having me train his staff.

Over the eight years I worked at the Keeble firm, I served as Project Manager for a number of larger and more prominent churches, along with several smaller but no less important ones, as well as several buildings of other types.

Among the most significant, at least to me, is First Baptist of Nashville. Located on a prominent corner of Broadway, Nashville's "High" street, in the center of town, this church had very limited land and an 1884 original building in poor shape. It was a large, imposing Victorian Gothic structure, magnificent and fitting for its day. However, the congregation had grown, and the ways of church practice had changed, when we began work on the project in 1965.

We started by doing a parallel study of two design options. One was an enlargement of the existing structure; the other a totally new building. At the end of that ten month study, it was shown that a new facility would cost only about $100,000 more than enlarging the old one, and that the result of following the enlargement option would be an awkward and difficult mixture of building technologies, possibly unsolvable building code issues, and a visual and spatial compromise. In choosing to erect a new building the Church and especially those favoring preservation were no doubt swayed by Keeble's inspired notion of retaining the tower from the 1884 building, admittedly suggested by Sir Basil Spence's Coventry Cathedral and several other European churches severely damaged by WWII bombings, and similarly restored, leaving towers or other remnants standing.

Keeping the tower led to an inquiry into the idea of the gothic idiom updated, and that is what we did. Thoroughly modern in its handling of materials and detailing, in its basic formal character it nonetheless reflects back to the gothic roots of the original building. While we had not heard of the term at that time, some might call it Postmodern. Keeble didn't like to use style names, and was heard to say that no building should have a style name applied to it until the architect had been dead for100 years.

To illustrate how far architects sometimes go to refine a design and to bring the client into the process, we engaged in some rather inventive and out-of-the-ordinary activities. For instance, Keeble engaged Goode Davis, a prominent Nashville portrait artist whose color sense he admired, to design the stained glass windows, something Davis had never done before. These windows are in the medium known as "faceted glass," and were fabricated and installed by the Willetts Studio of Philadelphia. Davis had produced transparencies of his proposed designs, executed at 1" = 1'-0" scale. To give the Building Committee the full impact of the large central window, to be located behind the Baptistry, using corrugated cardboard, we built an interior model of the chancel end of the Sanctuary at that same scale, with the window mounted in its correct place. It filled the end of the room where we set it up, in a space that could be made entirely dark. We positioned seats for the Committee so that their eyes would be at the same place a person's eyes would be when sitting on the front row of the Balcony in the real room. We led the Committee into the darkened room, sat them down, started playing a recording of a Bach organ cantata, and turned the lights on. There was soft general lighting, and the window was back-lit. In today's parlance, we knocked their socks off!

The Committee was elated, and we had no trouble getting approval for the design. We also built full-size cardboard models of the pulpit and the Lord's Table for the Committee's approval. Seating some two thousand, construction began in 1965 and was completed in 1970. A dedication service was held on Easter of that year, after I had moved to Chattanooga. When we started on this project I was not yet registered to practice architecture. I received my registration in 1968, two years before the building was completed.

Dr. W. A. Harrell, who was head of the BSSB Church Architecture Department, led the Building Committee sub-committee dealing with design. He was concerned that other churches would tend to copy this building. This church was considered by some to be the "Mother Church" of the Southern Baptist Convention, and it should be the best example in design we could make it. By all accounts it succeeds on this score and any others I have heard expressed. Dr. Harrell and I became strong friends, and when he died many years later, I was honored by being asked by his family to serve as a pallbearer.

The building design for First Baptist of Nashville won a design award at a conference on church architecture, sponsored by the Church Architecture Department of the Baptist Sunday School Board, in 1968.

Figure 12-2: First Baptist Church, Nashville, Tennessee, Exterior

Figure 12-3: First Baptist Church, Nashville, Tennessee, Interior

Other churches I worked on while with Keeble include Immanuel Baptist and Judson Baptist, both in Nashville. Both have sequels in my long practice.

At Immanuel our 1968 project was the addition of a new Sanctuary and Fellowship Hall, added to an original building designed by the firm of Hart Freeland Roberts, Inc., or HFR, in the 1950s. HFR had also designed, in 1913, an earlier building for Immanuel at another site, near downtown Nashville. The land for the newer church, located in the upscale area of Nashville known as Belle Meade, had been the home site of a Malone family. Their house had also been designed by HFR, and had been adapted by the church as the church office wing. In 1986 Orr/Houk, my firm, designed a new office addition, replacing the Malone house. In 2001 Orr/Houk merged with HFR. Things had come full circle.

Meanwhile, our family was continuing to grow. Early in our marriage, Nancy said that she wanted six children. I didn't say yea or nay, but I thought that number might be a wee bit high. When Nancy was pregnant with Mark, we discovered that she and I had an RH blood factor incompatibility. We were told that there shouldn't be any problems with the first child, but problems would become progressively more likely with each successive pregnancy. Steve was not planned, but we were thrilled when we found out he was on the way. He had a minimal problem from the RH factor; he had to have his blood exchanged in the hospital right after he was born, but otherwise he was perfect in every way. Doctors advised us to not have any more children. Late in 1964 we decided to look into adoption, and in the spring of 1965, to our delight, Karen arrived. She was only four weeks old, and beautiful. Three years later, we decided to adopt a second girl. Our beautiful Amy arrived in November of 1968, after being in foster care for four months for observation to see if a minor muscle problem would work itself out. It did, and again, we were blessed. All of our children, and now our grandchildren, eleven strong at last count, have continued to bless us again and again. Not to say that there haven't been rough times, but all in all, we are truly thankful.

In January 1968 our family moved into a house on Glendale Place in the Green Hills area of Nashville. Our next-door neighbors to the north were Sara and Elbridge White. I was in the midst of preparing to take the architectural registration exam, and Elbridge, a prominent architect, happened to be on the State Board of Examiners. He was very helpful, though he certainly didn't break any rules. He would have been just as helpful to anyone who had the same access to him I had. Elbridge became a great friend, architectural competitor, and later on, colleague. He was a partner at HFR and one of their primary design architects; and his presence was a strong reason that I felt comfortable merging our firm with HFR in 2001, although he was not there at that time. He retired in 1993 and died in 2000. In 1988 he and I teamed up with the late Charley Warterfield, FAIA, another premier Nashville architect, to edit a book, <u>Notable Nashville Architecture, 10930 - 1980</u>, published in 1989 by the local chapter of the American Institute of Architects.

The architectural registration exam, referred to briefly as the ARE, was different in those days from what it is today. Then it was given only twice a year, at a designated place, over four grueling days, terminating with a twelve-hour building design problem on the last day. One did everything by hand, making true or false or multiple-choice selections, working out mathematical problems and filling out answer sheets, or designing and drawing. There were seven parts, and if you passed as many as four parts you had to take the other three at the next cycle. You were given a limited number of tries to pass all parts; if you failed in that you had to start over.

Today, it has nine parts and is given by computer, and each part can be taken individually at almost whatever schedule the candidate wishes. The design problem, what some of us believe to be the heart of what architecture is truly about, has disappeared. Design skills are now tested in a series of very narrowly proscribed "vignettes." While the content of the exam may be more comprehensive today, those of us who had the old-style exam believe there is a value in dealing with the pressure of that short time span, and arriving at a comprehensive and coordinated design. Current candidates seem not to be tested for these qualities in the ARE today.

I sat for the Architectural Registration Examination in the summer of 1968, at the Engineering School at Vanderbilt University. One day in September of that year, when I arrived home, Elbridge called out to me from his front porch and asked me to come over for a minute. He told me that I had passed the examination and congratulated me. It meant an awful lot to hear that news directly from him.

Judson Baptist Church was a relocation project. At Keeble's we master-planned the site and designed an initial project consisting of an A-frame Sanctuary and an educational wing, connected only by a covered walkway. Like most of the churches I have worked with throughout my career, Judson had limited funds, and the scope of this initial project was all they could afford. What we designed and helped them build accommodated their space needs at the time. This project was completed in 1968. Over the ensuing years various other designers constructed three other additions, some not particularly visually compatible. One of these added to the education wing and completed an enclosed connector to the original Sanctuary, by then renamed the Chapel, because a new Sanctuary had been added around 1980. In 1996 Orr/Houk was hired to remodel this second Sanctuary. This included a totally new heating, ventilating and air conditioning system (HVAC), refinishing every exposed material in the room, even the pews, plus we made design changes that have resulted in a more visually unified and functional interior Two years later we were asked to produce a new master plan for the site, now enlarged by the acquisition of two additional parcels of land.

Figure 12-4: Judson Baptist Church,
Nashville, Tennessee, 1968 Relocation, Exterior

Alabama Boy

Figure 12-5: Judson Baptist Church,
Nashville, Tennessee, 1968 Relocation, Interior

Figure 12-6: Judson Baptist Church, Nashville, Tennessee,
1980 Sanctuary interior before renovation

One church project very important to me during those years is the First Christian Church of Glasgow, Kentucky. Completed in 1964, this relocation is the most radical church design of any I worked on at Keeble's, and probably in my entire career. I don't believe either Keeble or I or anyone at the firm had heard of Le Corbusier's Ronchamp Chapel at that time, but superficially this building strongly resembles it. There is nothing symmetrical in it in any way. The interior walls are brick (as they are at First Baptist, Nashville). The plan and section open out from the pulpit end in a sort of horn fashion, with slightly overlapping wall planes, some curved, ending in an all-glass end wall, looking out over a meadow. The roof sweeps up in a gracious curve, sloped at the wide end, with the higher corner pointing to a tall, open, tripod-like tower, which punctuates and anchors the overall exterior design. There are non-matching educational wings on either side of the Sanctuary. The

Figure 12-7: Judson Baptist Church, Nashville, Tennessee, 1980 Sanctuary interior after renovation

choir and organ are in the Balcony, and the natural acoustics are so good that most of the time no sound amplification is needed. It is smaller than some of the other churches we designed at Keeble's, seating only about 450. We have been told that it is in frequent demand for weddings.

An important lesson was driven home for me by what happened after one of our church projects had been completed and occupied, a Church of Christ in Sparta, Tennessee. Like many if not most, evangelical churches, money was limited, and we tried to be as frugal as possible in the design. This addition, a new Auditorium, is in the traditional basilica form, with a tall central nave and lower side aisles. The air conditioning is provided by two units located on either side of the Platform end, that blow air out toward the pews, plus a third unit under the Balcony.

Figure 12-8: First Christian Church,
Glasgow, Kentucky, Exterior

The Church called about a year after occupancy, complaining that the air conditioning system was not doing its job, and making so much noise that they had to cut it off to be able to hear during services. Keeble sent our mechanical engineer, up there to check things out. Returning, he reported that the Church had done absolutely no maintenance since they moved in. He found that the fan belt on one of the front units was broken, which meant that the motor was just spinning, not accomplishing anything. The Church had not changed filters on any of the units, and the unit under the Balcony was fully blocked. The other front unit was blocked also, and as a result, the return duct, in trying to pull air in, was "oil-canning," or popping in and out, making awful noises each time it popped. Our engineer, Hank Waechter, got the Church straightened out and committed to proper maintenance.

Figure 12-9: First Christian Church, Glasgow, Kentucky, Interior

I have taken this experience to every church project I have done since, "designing in" every conceivable means of minimum maintenance that I could, both in mechanical and other systems and in interior and exterior finishes.

We also try not to leave our church clients with the prospect of having to repaint exterior trim every few years. We try not to specify any high-maintenance materials on the exterior of our church buildings, recognizing that in many, if not most, churches maintenance is a sometimes thing. Where budgets are tight and churches rely heavily on volunteers for things like maintenance, everybody's business often becomes nobody's business, and it just doesn't get done. Instead of wood which will need painting sooner or later, we use brick, stone, factory-finished metals, and similar low or zero maintenance products for all exterior surfaces.

Another Alabama architectural experience from the Keeble years occurred in my hometown of Athens, at what was then Athens College. Then owned by the United Methodist Church, it has since been acquired by the State of Alabama, and is now named Athens State College. When I arrived at Keeble's office, he had a project under construction there, a dormitory. I had nothing to do with that, but later we were asked to design a rather large gymnasium, and he allowed me to serve as the Project Manager and take the design lead on it. This building has offices, locker rooms and other support spaces on the main floor, along with the gymnasium space itself. On a lower level, with on-grade access on the opposite side, is an enclosed swimming pool. It was an interesting design challenge for someone as green as I was, and I learned a lot from the experience.

Later at Athens College came the conversion of a true ante bellum house, of which there are many in Athens, into faculty apartments, without ruining this architectural treasure. I believe we succeeded.

During this time I augmented our income by designing, on my own, three more houses for friends in Athens. They weren't big money makers, though. I charged four cents a square foot. However, they gave me a little wider range of experience, as they were smaller and more modest than any Keeble's office are likely to have done.

In addition, I developed a sideline of drawing pastel portraits, mostly of friend's kids. I always worked from life, doing a quick sketch with the subject, and taking it home to produce the finished piece. In more recent years I have developed the habit of drawing pen-and-ink sketches of buildings and scenes on my travels. Sometimes I have been asked by a family member to draw a sketch of a building from a photograph, which I have done reluctantly. I would rather draw from life, and resist most opportunities to use photographs. When I have succumbed and used a photograph, the result usually turns out looking stale and dead.

In addition to a number of houses and churches, other buildings I was responsible for at Keeble's include three at The University of The South, at Sewanee, Tennessee. This campus is located on Monteagle Mountain in southeast Tennessee, about forty miles from

Chattanooga. The first of these is McCready Hall, a neo-gothic style dormitory on the main campus.

Later we were asked to produce a master plan for the sub-campus of the then-named Sewanee Military Academy, or SMA, an all-male prep school. From that effort came the commissions to design first, Cravens Hall, a dining hall with access from grade on the campus side, and an assembly hall below, with on-grade access from the boundary street on the opposite side. The assembly hall has a stage at one end, with an alter recess which can be screened off at the rear. This has an altar table and other liturgical fixtures, and a brilliant custom-designed faceted glass window, lit by natural light from an opening in the face of the kitchen loading dock above. The other building I designed is Hamilton Hall, a large classroom and administration building.

Both of these SMA buildings are thoroughly modern in design. All three of our Sewanee buildings feature the local fieldstone known as "Sewanee Stone," used as a virtual mandate on almost every University of the South building. In design we relied heavily on the stone as a dominant exterior material. By crafting forms that are in sync with the neo-gothic vocabulary of the existing buildings, reflecting their rhythms and massing while retaining our commitment to the principles of modern design, we were able to design these buildings thoroughly compatible with the rest of the campus. SMA was later merged with another boarding school and moved off-campus. The SMA buildings have been reassigned to the University Divinity School, and have recently been joined by a new chapel designed by the late Faye Jones, FAIA.

Near the middle of the top of Monteagle Mountain, and about seven or eight miles east of Sewanee, is the village of Monteagle, home of the Monteagle Assembly, a Chautauqua-like development started in the late1800s. The Keeble family had a home there, and he was born there. There remains a strong community of families with homes at "The Assembly," as it is familiarly known. Some of the houses date back into the 19th century, and have remained in the same families ever since. In the 1940s Keeble designed an exquisite small chapel on the grounds there, and it received rather wide publicity in the architectural press. During my stay with his firm, we designed a dining hall there. Mrs. Keeble's family also had a house on the Assembly grounds, and this had become the family's second home by the time I came to know them.

On two occasions my family was invited to stay there over a weekend. It is a delightful place and we thoroughly enjoyed both visits. One of these was in late spring and the forsythia was super abundant and glorious. We were able to visit the writer and scholar, Andrew Lytle, at his house in the Assembly. The Keeble house, named "Morningside," is still in that family. On another occasion I met the noted poet, Allen Tate, in Monteagle.

During my time with Keeble, I worked on a number of church projects, plus several houses, some of which were rather large and elaborate, and a variety of other projects. I also worked on a dormitory and a student center at Cumberland College, now Cumberland University, in Lebanon, Tennessee, and on H. G. Hill Elementary School in Nashville. Most of these were completed before I became registered or licensed as an architect.

All in all, my time with the Keeble firm turned out to be one of the broadest learning experiences and best internships anyone could ask for. In addition to all this professional experience, the importance of basic integrity was vigorously upheld. One event, while seemingly insignificant, illustrates this. The office had a coffee pot with payment on the honor system, five cents a cup. One day when I went to the pot to get a cup, another employee was just filling his cup and turned to leave without paying. I challenged him to pay up like the rest of us, and he said something to the effect that he didn't have to abide by such "silly" rules! This person was, until that time, a friend, and I was appalled. My thought was that he had "sold his soul" for only a nickel. I vowed that I would never "sell my soul" for any amount, and would try to never compromise my integrity for any reason.

Edwin Keeble was a dominant force in Nashville architecture for over fifty years. He not only produced a large number of prominent and important buildings – homes, churches, government buildings, and facilities for education at Vanderbilt University and for public school systems — but also pioneered in several technical areas, such as energy conservation, years ahead of his time. An example is the Life and Casualty Building, completed in 1957. This is a 31 story tower, at the time the tallest in the South, and unique in it's concepts and application of the principles of physics to achieve optimum savings of energy. As in all good and authentic architecture, these measures informed the design of the building. In the survey of architects for the book, <u>Notable Nashville Architecture</u>, the L&C received the highest favorable rating of any of the forty-some buildings included in the book, and by a wide margin.

13.

A TRANSITION

How many architects does it take to change a light bulb?

What's an architect?

*B*y 1969 it began to be obvious to me that I had reached the top of my potential at the Keeble firm, known in shorthand as EAK. At the State AIA (American Institute of Architects) convention that year I met Jack Tyler, a Chattanooga architect. Through conversations with him the idea emerged that I might go to work for him and his elderly partner, Mario Bianculli. After considerable thought and study I agreed and turned in my resignation at EAK, effective the end of December 1969. We visited Chattanooga several times prior to the move and bought a house under construction on Elder Mountain, west of town. Also known as Rattlesnake Mountain, this is actually in the next county. We scheduled a move on New Years Eve, and it snowed, though not enough to delay things. A delay did occur, though, because after loading all our goods, the moving van broke an axle or some such, and we had to wait almost a day while that was repaired. We did finally arrive and moved in, amidst snow and mud, and I reported for work on the first workday of 1970.

I had met Mario, of course, in the visits and discussions before I arrived for work, but I hadn't realized that he wasn't really too happy with idea of me being there. The premise that Jack and I had discussed was that when Mario retired I would be groomed to replace him as Jack's partner. Trouble was, Mario had no plans to retire, and he let me know that in no uncertain terms. Still I stuck it out for eight months, until finally Mario told me that he wanted me to go. In other words I was fired. I looked around briefly for a job in Chattanooga and then turned back toward Nashville, where we had been happier and had so many more friends and business contacts. While there are things I learned there, neither Nancy nor I had been truly happy in this situation. The drive to work from the house was down a steep road that sometimes was blocked by rock slides. When that happened we had to use an old one-lane timber track, and sometimes met another car coming the other way, and one of us had to back up until we found a place to pull off. Living on the mountain was even harder on Nancy. She had to drive the boys to two different schools, one of which was on Lookout Mountain. That meant that the drive was down one mountain and up another, two ways, twice a day. We had made few friends in Chattanooga, and finally realized that we missed Nashville and our friends there.

One of those friends was, of course, Edwin Keeble. After looking into a few prospective jobs, Keeble, who had sold his practice to five of his former associates the previous spring, offered to help me set up my own practice. I was given the use of a small house he owned next door to his old office on Glen Echo Drive in the Green Hills section of Nashville, to use as an office and a weekday residence for me while the family and I looked for a permanent home. Also, he made me a modest loan, which, though it took me a long time, I eventually repaid. In exchange, he and I would collaborate on projects his friends brought to him; he would do the design and I would provide the other services. This phase of our association produced a couple of nice though modest houses, the renovation of the Parish Hall at Otey Parish Church, Episcopal in the town of Sewanee, and what became a rather extended multi-phase project at a bank in Winchester. It was a wonderful way for me to start a practice, and I will never be able to adequately express my gratitude for it. Keeble died in 1979 at the age of seventy-five. I still miss him and have tried to share with his family my thanks for all he did for me. Not only did he help me get started in my practice, he taught me practically everything I know about the nature and meaning of being an architect, the values and principles, the focus and passion and persistence being an architect takes. Largely due to Keeble's influence, over the course of my internship and practice I have learned many valuable lessons about design and the philosophy of architecture, about how to produce it, and thousands of technical and practical things. I have a goal of trying to learn some new thing every day. What Keeble taught me included many of these lessons, but more importantly, he taught me how to BE an "Architect."

Among those lessons I learned from Keeble is that an architect has an obligation to pass on to the next generation the lessons he has learned, to be a mentor to them. I have tried to do that in my practice, and in a way, in writing this book.

14.

STEPPING OUT

What's the best way to make a small fortune in architecture?

Start with a large one.

My very first project after setting up my practice as Frank Orr Architects (FOA) was a W. T. Grant store in Cookeville, Tennessee, brought to me by Tom Crain, a developer I had met during my Keeble days. It was to be basically an adaptation of one of Grant's standard plans, but it was work, and I needed it. A little later Crain hired me to design a small shopping center in Henderson, Kentucky. This gave me a little more design freedom, and more income. I was grateful. In addition, Keeble brought me the projects I described in the previous chapter.

My office officially opened in early September, 1970. In the meantime, Nancy and the children had to stay in Chattanooga, while I lived in the little house Keeble was lending me for an office.

In November we sold our house in Chattanooga and bought one in Nashville, and we all were together again. This Nashville house was a typical "Ranch Burger," roomy but without charm of any stripe. In addition, the yard was about two acres, with a grade drop of some one hundred feet from back to front. The ground was rocky.

I don't believe it had ever been given its final grading. Mowing was an absolute bear. Hate is not a very healthy emotion, but I came close to hating that house. Two and a half years later we found another house and moved.

In January, 1971, I moved my office to a circa 1915 house on West End Avenue, rented from Russell Brothers, who had been the Building Committee Chairman for the First Baptist Church project. I stayed there until the spring of 1976 when I moved to a small recently built office building on Sweetbriar Avenue. The second floor was unfinished shell space, and I made a deal with the owner, a personal friend, to design the build-out in exchange for rent for several months. He and a partner had hired me to master plan and design the buildings for a retirement housing development in the Bellevue area of Nashville. Now owned by Tennessee Baptist Adult Homes, Inc., it is named Deerlake, and it features some rather forward-thinking ideas for its time, both in site planning and in building design, particularly for dealing with accessibility needs. Many of these are considered standard practice today.

As I have mentioned, among the several projects Keeble brought me during the FOA years was a renovation of the Parrish Hall at Otey Parrish Church, Episcopal in Sewanee. During my first visit to the Church with Keeble, I had the distinct feeling I had met the Rector somewhere before. Finally, it got the best of me, and I asked him had he ever been associated with Auburn University. He replied that he had taught swimming in the PE Department there for several years – and had been my swimming instructor some twenty years earlier.

Other work came in, mostly as a result of contacts developed over the years. Very few, if any, just walked in the door. Contact with friends at the Baptist Sunday School Board (BSSB) led to several interesting and generally profitable projects. We did several Baptist Book Stores; some were renovations, but those most fulfilling for a designer were new buildings, all based on a standard design package, adapted to each site.

Figure 14-1: Baptist Book Store, Standard Design

These were built in some ten locations. In 1978 the AIA Research Corporation, in a nation-wide research project, engaged us to produce a conceptual re-design of the store in Raleigh, North Carolina, attempting to minimize energy consumption. Altogether there were around 160 projects like ours in this study. Ours was one of only two designed by Tennessee architects. Realizing that operating hours for a bookstore were mostly in the daytime, we focused on daylighting as a primary strategy for saving energy. In developing our redesign, we built an interior model, and using a light meter, tested it in sunlight in several places inside, taking readings for particular times of the day and dates of the year, predicting the performance for a real, full-size building. Our calculations showed that the energy savings were huge, so high they were "off the scale." In our report we modestly pegged them at fifty percent. We worked with mechanical and electrical engineers on this research. I have tried to apply the lessons learned from this exercise, but unfortunately, until recently there was little interest among our clients to conserve energy. The one exception was the

Baptist Pavilion at the 1982 World's Fair in Knoxville, which is described in a later chapter.

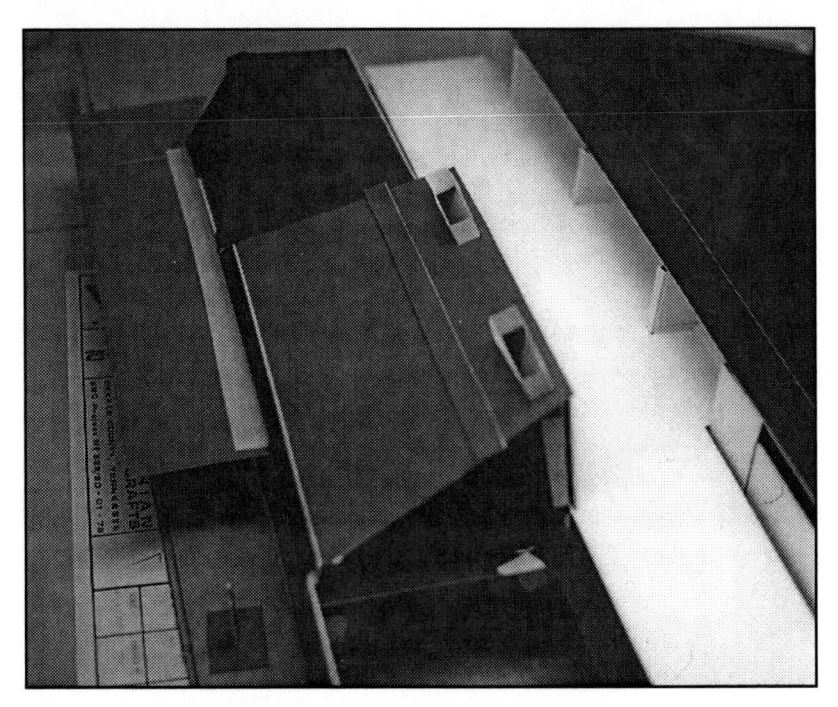

Figure 14-2: Baptist Book Store, Standard Design, redesigned for maximum energy conservation

In more recent years this movement has been labeled, "Sustainability," and encompasses more than just saving energy. It also includes air quality, improved productivity, conservation of resources, and minimizing maintenance. Studies have shown that, while the initial cost for these choices may be higher than more conventional construction, there are savings in costs in the long term, over the life cycle of a building.

When I started practice, I was convinced that there had to be a better way of determining compensation for architectural services than the traditional percentage of construction method, which is what we had always used at Keeble's office. In researching, this I found that there are several other plans, and I experimented with some of them for some time before settling on the fixed-sum method as my standard. While I believe this is the most fair to both client and architect, it is hard to calculate the proper fee for services. The architect has to be careful and skilled in negotiation to avoid risks he should not face.

One project Keeble brought to me drove this home. It was an addition to a historic log house, and the owner was a lady of substantial wealth and high visibility in the community. The contractor provided all the materials for the project except the logs, discarded from old tobacco pens, which the owner had purchased independently. Tobacco pens were log buildings early settlers used for curing tobacco. They were usually about twenty feet square, and the logs, some being over one hundred years old and well seasoned, are highly valued for re-use in new log buildings.

Because of Keeble's involvement, we had used the percentage method to determine the fee. When it came time to settle up, we submitted a bill calculated on the Contractor's costs plus what was considered to be a fair market value for the logs. The Owner objected, saying that because she had bought the logs they shouldn't be figured in the fee calculation. I tried to explain that we had to include the logs in the design of the addition, and that it was standard practice to include them in the bill as if the contractor had furnished them. She still argued, and I continued to stand my ground. The difference in the fee was only a little over $900.

Finally, she asked if it would it be all right if she paid it off at $100 a month; this from a woman who could have written a check to cover the entire city payroll for a month if she had wanted. I agreed, but from that time on I decided that I would avoid at all costs using the percentage method, if for no other reason than to not have to face just such situations as this.

Another BSSB project was a package of three residential buildings at the Ridgecrest Baptist Conference Center in North Carolina. There were designed like motel rooms, treated visually to agree with the mountain rustic feel of the natural environment and the other buildings at the Center. In addition, we did several renovation projects at the BSSB headquarters building, scattered throughout that huge rambling compound. Included was a new executive suite for the President, occupying the entire eleventh floor of the central tower.

Figure 14-3: Maple Lodge,
Ridgecrest Baptist Conference Center, Ridgecrest, North Carolina

Even though I had been committed to the design of churches as a primary focus of my practice, other than the first of what would ultimately become four projects at Woodmont Baptist Church, described in more detail below, we designed only two church projects in the FOA years that were built.

One was a minor renovation at First Baptist of Cullman, Alabama, brought to us by Mama's sister Libby's family, members there. As is sometimes the case, the Pastor decided on his own to do something without getting the congregation's approval. What he had done was to authorize the demolition of an older wing that was no longer useful. Problem was, this left an ugly face, like an open wound, right on the main street of the town. Our task was to add a new façade and do some interior renovations and additions.

The other church project was a multipurpose building, a combination gym and fellowship hall, for Fifteenth Avenue Baptist, an African American congregation, the first of several church projects for non-white congregations. This was the result of the friendship with the Pastor, Rev. Enoch Jones, gained through an annual joint service our church had with 15th Avenue. Their folks would come to Woodmont and Rev. Jones would preach at the morning service. That evening our members would go to 15th Avenue and out pastor would preach. The actual building was not built until we became Orr/Houk, some years later. During the FOA period we also produced a master plan for First Baptist of Athens, but it was several years before a building came from it.

Master plans have become, over the years, an important part of our practice, especially for churches, but also for a variety of other clients and sites. Master plans for large tracts of land can take many forms and include a wide variety of project scope. It is not codified, and likely no two architectural firms will do it exactly the same way. Our approach and process begins with what we call "Visioning." We begin this by holding a two-to-three hour intense session with the Committee, the church staff, and key program leaders, something like a charrette, described below. In this we lead the group through a series of exercises that are designed to bring out the concerns, needs and dreams of the church, prioritize them, and try to help the group find concensus. The result of this then becomes a strategic work plan for the rest of the master plan tasks. In most of our master plans we include analyses of the site, the space program, and if the church has an existing building, the building itself. While every master plan may differ in content, our final product usually includes a report on how the results were generated, a set of recommendations, and estimates of probably costs, by phases if that was a part of the recommendations, all illustrated by drawings and tables, and recorded in a written report.

One of those non-church master plans is Clifftops, an 1,885 acre second-home development near Monteagle, Tennessee. This has some 215 five-acre lots, a small lake with marina, and other amenities usually found in these kinds of developments. Many of the lots are on bluffs, and overlook vast expanses of unspoiled nature. Some views are more than thirty miles long.

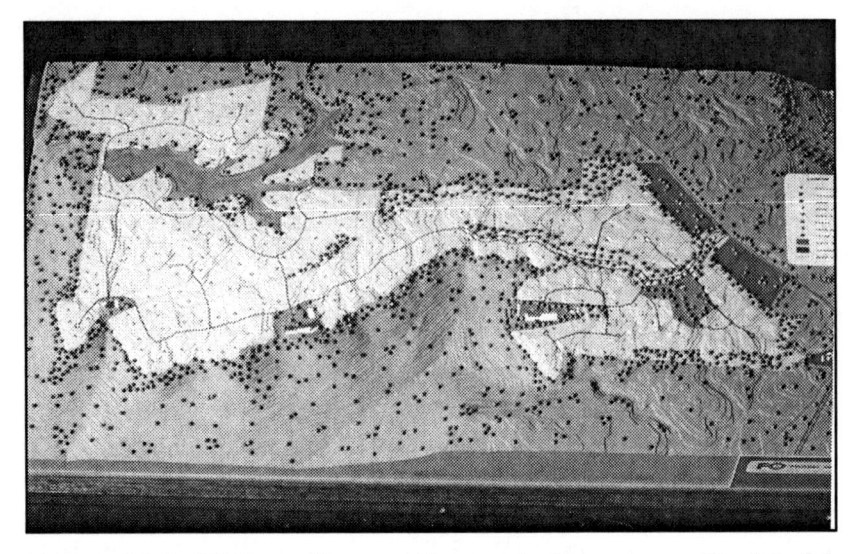

Figure 14-4: Clifftops Resort, Monteagle, Tennessee, Site Model

Architects, like all professionals, should engage in public service from time to time. I had the opportunity to serve on various AIA committees and in other professional roles. Some were local, some at the state level, some national. In the mid-1970's I was appointed to the National AIA Committee on Environmental Education, which I served on for four years. Meeting usually at the AIA headquarters in Washington, this committee was not charged with dealing with clean air and water, but rather with enhancing public awareness of and concern for the built environment, particularly among school-age children. I have also served on the Tennessee Society of Architects, now called AIA Mid-Tennessee, Board of Directors, and the local AIA chapter Board.

During the 1970s a movie theater in downtown Nashville burned down. It was located on Church Street opposite the south end of Capitol Boulevard, which is on an axis with the State Capitol Building to the north. The local AIA chapter decided to have the chapter perform an urban design study, using the opportunity of the hole in the city fabric where the theater had stood, to recommend a new urban plan for Nashville. Four very junior team leaders, of which I was one, were appointed, and each of us picked four or so other architects to make up our team. We kicked it off with a design charrette one Saturday. Later it was published in a book, but I am not aware of anything explicit that ever came of it.

The term "charrette" has an interesting history in architecture. It has come to mean an intense design effort attended by many people, often brought together to address a special civic concern. It can last all day, overnight or extend over several days. Originally, though, the word came from France, where tradition has it that it came from the name of a small two-wheeled donkey cart. The legend, now obscured by a century or more of the mists of time, was that Parisian architecture students labored all night in their homes on design assignments due the next day at the ateliers of their teachers, and in trying to get in the last possible minute, still at work on their projects, would be seen early in the morning, riding in these carts, with their drawing boards, hard at work, as they were driven to the atelier.

In the 1996 a new seven-lane arterial road was proposed by government transportation planners, crossing from east to west through the southern part of the Nashville business district. It was to be a limited-access thruway with the purpose of conveying traffic around the business district without having to be interrupted by it. It was to cut through the street grid, creating an impenetrable barrier between the two resulting parts, and it would have been terrible for the city. The AIA chapter convened an <u>ad hoc</u> group of six architects to look into this and see what could be done to stop or change it into something positive. I was honored to be included, along with Batey Gresham, Clay Hickerson, Ron Lustig, Bob Oglesby, and Seab Tuck. It is interesting to note that three of the six were Auburn grads – Gresham, Tuck, and me. We met several times, and conducted some activities and campaigns to alert the public about this. Things seemed to snowball. Our efforts began to show results. We were given a name, the Nashville Urban Design Forum. The weekly newspaper <u>The Nashville Scene,</u> and their staff architectural writer, Christine Kreyling, helped to organize a design charrette to explore the implications of a fresh urban design look at the area of the city that would be affected, named "South of Broadway," or "Sobro," for short. The end result of all this public attention was that the government changed the new road design to one that will be smaller (four lanes), slower, pedestrian-friendly, and will knit the urban fabric together rather than split it apart. I was out of town on one of our overseas trips during the charrette, but I fully support everything it proposed.

This all built up a lot of public interest in urban design and planning matters. The Urban Design Forum began to have a regular schedule of meetings, inviting the public, and offering courses in urban design and similar topics. Eventually, from this activity a permanent organization grew, the Nashville Civic Design Center, or NCDC, supported by the city, Vanderbilt University, and the University of Tennessee, and grants from foundations, and led by a senior architect professor, on leave from the University of Tennessee. It has been a very positive force in moving Nashville toward a city with a strong sense of the value of good urban planning, and of a gracious environment. One major project of the NCDC is a two-year-long study named The Plan of Nashville, or PoN. Patterned after the Plan of Chicago of a century ago, this comprehensive plan attempts to place before Nashville a vision of a future in which the best urban design is not only possible, but also desirable, and how to make it happen. I was rather deeply involved in the PoN, and am still active in the forum, and am very proud to have had the opportunity to participate in these efforts.

Another area of service architects sometimes engage in is teaching. It usually includes being paid, although usually a mere pittance. During two different periods I taught part-time at the O'More School of Design, a college-level school of interior design in Franklin, Tennessee. In addition, I taught evening courses for several terms at the Nashville Institute of Technology, commonly known as Nashville Tech. An old friend and Keeble colleague who was on full-time staff there at the time, brought me into this. After teaching one semester of a course titled, "Introduction to Architecture," I remarked to him that I didn't think much of the textbook we were using. His response was, "Well, why don't you write a better one?" I gave that some thought, and eventually did just that. It was titled Professional Practice in Architecture, and was published by Van Nostrand Reinhold in 1982. It was used at Nashville Tech and other, similar institutions until the material became outdated.

Nancy and I joined Woodmont Baptist Church when we first arrived in Nashville in 1962, and rejoined when we returned in 1970. In 1974 a fire gutted the church's original 1943 building, which by that time had become the church Chapel. My firm was hired to restore it. I was about to be engaged in one of the most significant events in my practice.

15.

ORR/HOUK

"Nothing in life is so exhilarating as being shot at without result."
Winston Churchill

*I*n the mid-1970s I began to realize that I was not a very good businessman, and was drifting deeper and deeper into debt. One of my smarter ideas to get out of this dilemma was to find a partner I could cajole into coming in with me, who had the business acumen and other management skills I lacked. Ed Houk was a member of Woodmont Baptist Church and on the Building Committee for the Chapel restoration. During the duration of that project, I got to know him well, and recognized in him the very qualities I was looking for in a partner. It took me over a year, but I finally convinced him to join me, and on November 1, 1976, Orr/Houk and Associates Architects, Inc. (O/H) was born.

Second only to convincing Nancy to marry me, this step was the smartest thing I have ever done. Ed probably thought it was the dumbest he had ever done, because, once there, he realized that things were very bad, financially and otherwise. We had too many people, more than our income could support. He slashed our staff, and he and I both took substantial salary cuts. Similar to the way Nancy and I complement each other, Ed and I have opposite but complementary traits while holding the same focus and purpose. He tends to worry over things while I am likely to shrug them off. That's probably why I got the firm in such bad financial straits to begin with. We struggled both as an office and individually, but through his discipline we survived, and ultimately thrived. I cannot express how much I owe Ed Houk. I hope he realizes the depth of my gratitude.

In addition to bringing Ed and me together, the initial Woodmont project was only the first of four there over the next several years. They seemed to follow about every five years. This experience and those with other churches led us to observe that a church looking into a building program should plan for the next five years. It takes roughly a year from the date the church decides it needs to expand to having the design process complete and ready for construction to begin. Then, the construction phase will take up to two years or so before the church can move in and begin to use the facility. That leaves the last two years of the five-year planning span for the church to grow into the capacity the building should have been designed for. You don't want the building to be full the day you move in, so you should provide some expansion capacity. Historically, it all works out to be roughly a five-year cycle, and the Woodmont experience proves that.

The second Woodmont project added a single-story education wing between the Sanctuary and the Chapel, plus a new choir rehearsal room at the rear of the Sanctuary. The education wing was structurally designed to carry two more future floors, and the third project added those, expanding the church offices and adding more education space. The last project, completed in 1989, was a three-story education wing, with preschool space on the lower two floors and adult space on the top floor.

Figure 15-1: Woodmont Baptist Church,
Nashville, Tennessee, 1979 Classroom Addition

Figure 15-2: Woodmont Baptist Church,
Nashville, Tennessee, 1983 Classroom and Office Addition

Figure 15-3: Woodmont Baptist Church, Nashville, Tennessee, 1987 Preschool Addition

Realizing that owning our own building rather than renting office space might be better in terms of financial health, long-range stability, and public visibility, Ed and I began to look for a building to own. In September 1980 we bought and moved into our own place, a 1915-era foursquare house at 1905 21st Avenue South in the Hillsboro Village area of Nashville. This stands as another very smart thing, one Ed and I did together. Even though O/H no longer exists, Ed and I still own this building. It has turned out to be a very wise investment.

In the combined years of practice as FOA and O/H, our work covered around eighty churches plus over forty other church-related projects. In addition, several other categories of project types can be named – over fifty master plans, almost fifty shoe stores, and a number of pro bono projects for religious and other non-profit organizations; all this plus a scattering of other building types.

The shoe stores present an interesting story. Beginning in 1978 we had been engaged by Genesco, a shoe manufacturer and retailer headquartered in Nashville, to design small shoe stores in various parts of the country. Some were in spaces previously occupied by either another Genesco store or by a different tenant. Some were in new spaces; almost all were in enclosed malls, though at least two were in open-air malls in more temperate zones, like Miami. They were for several different Genesco brands – Hardy, Jarman, Cover Girl, Bell Brothers, Flagg and Johnston and Murphy – some of which do not exist today. Genesco paid for our state architectural registrations where we designed the stores. Eventually we designed stores in twenty-one states, multiple times in some.

However, sometime in 1980 Genesco decided to set up their own in-house design studio, and ceased to give us any new projects. In 1981 the country was in a fairly deep recession, and it turned out to be a very down year for O/H. It got so bad that in the fall we were wondering if we would survive. We had no active work and nothing on the horizon. Ed and I having let everyone else in the firm go, began to plan to close the office and had started to pack up some things.

Ed has always had a rigid attitude toward financial matters. We always operated on a cash basis, and never went into debt other than to buy our building. He had declared that we would close the office when we had money for two month's salary for the two of us left in the bank, so that he and I would have that to live on while we looked for new jobs. We pegged December first as our drop-dead date for closing up. That date came and went as we, perhaps unrealistically, hung on, hoping for a miracle.

Then, about the middle of the month, our contact at Genesco called and asked if we were still in business. We assured him we were and were given two more shoe stores to design. Those two projects didn't generate much income, but they gave us enough to keep us going through the next February, and by then more work had come in, and we never looked back. One way to look at this would be to say that we had been "shot at without result." In another way it might be said that the Lord was asking us if we were willing to give up what we had worked so hard to build if He asked us to. We apparently passed the test; we were willing to give it all up; but fortunately didn't have to.

Architectural design competitions are a way owners of high-profile projects are able to involve a large number of architects in the early design process, and a way for relatively unknown architects to try to secure highly prized commissions. There are criticisms of this process, and most are justified. For one thing it prevents the architect from having meaningful, beneficial contact and interaction with the users of the facility. However, competitions are attractive, and for some, including me, they offer opportunities to spread our design wings in ways our usual practices do not. For this reason, rather than for any realistic hope of winning, I have entered several design competitions. Most were of the type I described above, with little expectation of winning. A few have had somewhat more potential for success. One of those was for the design of a new multipurpose arena for Nashville. We helped put together a team consisting of HKS, a nationally known firm from Dallas with extensive experience in this kind of facility, plus another Nashville architectural firm, Hickerson-Fowlkes, various engineering and specialty consultants, and Orr/Houk. We didn't win but were in the final five. Later at HFR I participated, without success, in the design competition for the Grand Egyptian Museum in Cairo.

There was one competition we did win though, and by ourselves. This was for new first-class lodge facilities at two conference centers owned by Tennessee Baptists, Carson Springs and Linden Valley. Both of these sites had been developed in the 1940s by Tennessee Baptists as summer youth camps. The owners desired to add to them the capability to serve as adult conference centers, and our new facilities were designed to accomplish that goal. The building at Linden Valley has 40 rooms and a multi-functional meeting center. Carson Springs has 36 rooms with expansion capacity for at least 36 more, plus a meeting facility twice as large as Linden Valley, and a 300-seat dining hall.

Figure 15-4: Carson Springs Baptist Conference Center, Newport, Tennessee, Exterior

Alabama Boy

Figure 15-5: Carson Springs Baptist Conference Center,
Newport, Tennessee, Interior

We tended to stay away from government projects at O/H. During the FOA period, largely due to the efforts of Earl Durard, one of my employees who had political connections, we were awarded a contract by the State of Tennessee to design a new center for the study of crafts. The state had then, and still maintains, a policy of awarding design contracts for projects costing over a certain limit to architectural joint ventures, and usually dictates who the partners will be. We were to be teamed with Jim Franklin, a well-known and well-connected architect from Chattanooga. Jim and I met a couple of times and he proposed that we divide the work and the fee in a way that put my work and consequently my part of the fee at the rear end of the process, meaning it might be years before I received any substantial money for the project, or maybe never, because some projects never materialize. I sent word that this was not acceptable, and we were authorized to proceed with the preliminary design alone. When that phase was complete, the project was set aside for several months, during which time Congressman Joe L. Evins secured Federal funding for it through the Appalachian Regional Commission. By the time the project became active again it had been moved from its original site on the Natchez Trace in Williamson County to a new site on a peninsula on Center Hill Lake in DeKalb County, in Evins' Congressional district. Also, a new joint venture was imposed on us, this time with another Nashville firm, Cain- Schlott. By that time, though, we had become the lead architect and could craft a more attractive division of work and fee than had been the case earlier. The Governor named it the Joe L. Evins Applachian Center for Crafts, or the Appalachian Crafts Center for short.

In keeping with the crafts theme of the facility, the team – owner and designers — decided to use custom-cast bells in lieu of a traditional dedication plaque. These were cast by Morris Parker, an architect and foundryman, who learned his craft at Solari's Arcosanti establishment in Arizona. Now hung over the fireplace in the Lobby of the main building, three bells make up a mobile, with the usual dedication text cast into them. There for all the world to see, for however long they stay there, is my name on the same bell as a former Governor who spent time in jail after leaving office.

Figure 15-6: Joe L. Evins Appalachian Crafts Center, DeKalb County, Tennessee

However, in terms of profitability the Crafts Center was a disaster. I am sure we lost huge amounts of money on it. We had to put up with untold reams of red tape, as well as dealing with governmental indecision and changes of minds. Even though it turned out to be a very nice facility, the Appalachian Crafts Center simply was not a financially viable and sensible venture, and we swore we would never again become involved in a state project. Fortunately, we were able to capitalize on the experience of designing that kind of facility later. We cited the Crafts Center in the qualifications we submitted that led to the Tennessee Baptist lodges projects.

Jim Franklin remains a friend. He later moved to Washington and served on staff at the AIA headquarters, and was inducted into the AIA College of Fellows (FAIA). More recently he has been on the faculty of a school of architecture in California.

We didn't swear off government work entirely, though. Back in the FOA days I had been given a project with the Metro Nashville School Board, a small renovation of an under- utilized area of the Eakin Elementary School building, converting it into satellite offices for the district staff. After that was completed, I was asked if I wanted to take on another small renovation at another school. For some reason that I cannot at this stage comprehend, I declined. It was many years later before we, then O/H, got another chance to do work for the School Board. The project was a new building for an existing elementary school, Harpeth Valley. It was a replacement of a building that had initially been built in the late 1930s, and cluttered up in the intervening years with awkward, ill-advised additions and portable classrooms. We began design in 1988, and completed construction documents on schedule, but the project was put on hold for budgetary reasons. Then, in 1991, it was resurrected, but the plans had to be revised to accommodate changes in the Board's standard grade allocation structure, and the new demographics of its area. It went from a K-6 to a K-4 school. As intended, it was bid and came in within budget, and construction began.

During construction, a happy thing occurred. The School Board hired a management firm, Heery, Inc., to oversee their construction program, and the Heery employee having responsibility for our project was David Gilpin, who had been working in Keeble's office the day I joined that firm. He had continued there after I left, and he and I had kept in loose contact over the years.

Harpeth Valley was a particularly successful project. It was built behind the old existing building, which was then demolished. That created a large front yard, providing adequate room for the parents' drop-off and pick-up driveway, and for staff and visitor parking, as well as a gracious lawn. It features an interior courtyard, and a complete circulation loop around through all the classroom wings. Such a pattern allows ease of traffic in either direction from any point to any other. This concept is one I have always promoted in our church design, one that is especially useful when there are large numbers of people in a building, who have to move about often and all at the same time, as they do in schools and churches.

Figure 15-7: Harpeth Valley Elementary School, Nashville. Tennessee

Like most other government bodies, the School Board has a policy of "spreading out" the design contracts, in other words, awarding them to as many different architects as possible. Surprisingly, we were given the contract to design another elementary school in relatively short order. We knew that Harpeth Valley had been very popular with principals and staff, but were not expecting another commission so soon. The new project was for Hickman Elementary School, another replacement but at a new site. The site was difficult. It was carved off of that of a former high school that was being converted by another architectural firm into a middle school. The land left over for the elementary school is rather long and narrow and has a substantial slope across it. The Board wanted almost a duplicate of Harpeth Valley, but that simply was not feasible. We did manage to have another central courtyard and circulation loop, however, and everyone seems to find it successful.

The School Board has a provision in their design contracts allowing them to reuse construction documents for one of their buildings for another school, paying the architect half the original fee. We were asked to do this at a new site for an entirely new school in the Antioch area of Nashville, using the Hickman plans. After some time trying to make this work, we determined, and the Board agreed, that due to the particulars of the site chosen, it wasn't feasible, and once again we were given a contract for a new school building. Because of the site conditions, this building does not have a courtyard, and it is has two stories, while the other two have only one story. When we began it did not have a name, but by the time construction began it was named the Henry C. Maxwell Elementary School. This was a particularly interesting, but perhaps not surprising development, considering that in some ways Nashville is not such a large town after all. It turned out that Mr. Maxwell was the father of Rev. Bruce Maxwell, the pastor of one of our most important church projects. Rev. Maxwell's church is the Lake Providence Missionary Baptist Church, an African American congregation, about which more will be said later.

These schools and the Crafts Center were the only government projects we did, either as FOA or O/H. While the Crafts Center was certainly not an experience we wanted to repeat, the schools were quite nice for us. The people we worked with on them were congenial, cooperative, decisive and considerate, and the projects were reasonably profitable. My relationship with Dave Gilpin and his role in these school projects no doubt played a big part in the success they had. We would have been glad to continue to do more schools for them, but our good fortune in having more than our share of commissions in a short length of time had run out. By the time Maxwell School was completed O/H had merged with Hart Freeland Roberts, Inc. which had also had its share of school projects.

There were a small number of sort of quasi-public projects we did in the FOA years. These were historic restoration packages at Belmont Mansion in Nashville and Oaklands, a similar house museum in Murfreesboro. Though funded in part by state matching grants, our clients were the owners of the houses, and so officially these were private projects.

There is one _pro bono_ project worthy of special note. This is the Baptist Pavilion at the 1982 Worlds Fair in Knoxville. Our Client was an _ad hoc_ group of Baptist agencies organized to respond to this unique opportunity. Built around a simple pre-engineered metal shed roof shell, it enclosed a small multi-media theater and several exhibits. A special new musical and mixed media show was crafted and presented several times a day during the six-month run of the fair. On the exterior we added fabric banners that wrapped up one side, over the roof, and down the other side. These had three functions; one, to shade the roof from the sun, addressing the energy-saving theme and focus of the fair, two, giving the rather mundane basic building a more distinctive profile, and three, creating a Christian flag when seen from above, as from the overhead cable car that traversed the fair site. We feel that this was one of our most important efforts, because more than eleven million people visited the fair, and if one-tenth of them visited the Pavilion, it resulted in a massive presentation of the Christian message. Surprisingly, after the fair closed and all exhibit structures were supposed to be razed, the Pavilion was purchased by the Tennessee Baptist Convention, dismantled and re-erected for use as an activities building at their conference center site at Linden, Tennessee, where later we designed a new lodge.

Most of our _pro bono_ projects we never saw; we neither visited the site before construction nor the building during or after construction. We simply had to rely on information given to us by the clients. Sometimes we saw photos of the completed building, but more often not even that. Among those in this category are a conference center in Benin, churches in Panama and Sierra Leone, and a denominational headquarters building in Canada.

Even though my personal practice has always been focused on religious architecture, that is certainly not all we worked on. During the FOA years, we designed several houses, and a few during the O/H period. After a while though, Ed and I agreed that neither of us was really temperamentally well equipped to deal with that kind of client, and we decided that as long as other kinds of work were available we would turn down any more house projects, and refer any such opportunities to other architects. We also determined that there are some projects to which we have moral objections, and that we would pass on them as well. One somewhat vague possibility, coming to us through a relative of Ed's wife, Kaye, was the opportunity to be considered for the design of a large casino and resort complex in the Smoky Mountains area, to be owned by the Cherokee Indians. Believing that gambling is not good for anyone, not to mention committed Christians, after wrestling with our consciences a couple of days, we decided to turn it down.

The second major building type that consumed much of our time and effort falls into the general category of healthcare. Ed's background before joining me had been almost totally in healthcare design, and through his contacts, beginning in 1981, we provided services continually to a private healthcare development company for several years. The first project was a new 44-bed hospital in Linden, Tennessee, the Perry Memorial Hospital. This was followed by three other new hospitals of similar size, located in Tennessee, Kentucky, and Virginia, plus a dozen or more additions and renovations in a wide variety of locations. Hospitals and shoe stores are about as different as any two building types could be, but I believe we did both well.

There was, however, an even larger body of work that personally I was involved in only marginally. In 1985, nine years after O/H began and after nine years of persistent marketing by Ed, we got our first project at Vanderbilt University Medical Center, or VUMC, located only a few blocks from our office, practically within walking distance. The project was a very small blood bank in one room in the existing hospital complex. In the remaining years of

O/H we were never without an active project at VUMC. With only a couple of exceptions, all of our projects at Vanderbilt were interior renovations of existing spaces. Some were clinics of various types, some were administrative offices, and a few were for unique functions. However, the large majority of these projects were research laboratories.

The largest and most unique of these was the addition of, in effect, five new floor levels built on top of an existing six-story building. Ed has become a nationally recognized expert in the design of research labs. At the time of the Hart Freeland Roberts, Inc. (HFR) merger, O/H had designed 148 individual projects for VUMC. At HFR Ed has continued to work almost exclusively on VUMC projects.

Figure 15-8: Werthan Building Expansion,
Vanderbilt University Medical Center, Nashville, Tennessee

Sometime in 1984 a fellow walked into the office and wanted us to design a small office building to be located on Nashville's Music Row. He was very specific about some things, primarily that it had to have an exterior skin of a recently developed technology using what is called four-way structural glass. This system utilizes large glass panels without visible exterior structural supports, either vertical or horizontal, creating an almost seamless surface. The owner also wanted to have a small amount of some more natural material on the building to link it to the rural character of the music industry. In response we designed the two public entrances with stone.

Figure 15-9: Merit Music Building, Nashville, Tennessee

Many of our church design projects were preceded by separate master plans of their sites. We took great pains to involve the church leadership and the congregations at large, because we had learned that if the membership was involved they would have an investment in the process, take ownership in it, and would be more likely to be supportive when it came time to put the recommendations into action. This process has been described in more detail earlier. We believe that it is prudent to produce a report complete enough so that anyone in the Church who had not been a part of the process could pick up a copy and fully understand how the results were generated.

In a few cases we were not allowed to follow through with the building design project after the master plan was completed. Sometimes the church simply did not believe they had the resources to proceed, or sadly lacked the will to make the bold moves it frequently takes in matters of faith.

However, there were some master planning projects that did move ahead without our further involvement. Usually this occurred with churches at some distance away, when the churches wanted to have the design architects closer to home. One such, of which we feel that our master plan was especially successful, was for the First Baptist Church of Pasadena, Texas, which was unique in several ways. For one thing, we almost never did any mass mailing for marketing, and this was our only success from this kind of effort. We had found a list of churches that had sent attendees to a recent BSSB conference for very large churches, focusing on the unique problems and opportunities such churches faced. We sent out blind mailings to them, stating our interest and qualifications. There was no immediate response, but several months later FBC Pasadena called us. They were planning to relocate to a new, undeveloped, forty-nine acre site. We had worked on relocations and undeveloped sites before, but this was a long way from home, and we had to become familiar with the topography and local regulations. Working closely with the church, we developed a long-range concept featuring parallel corridor spines into which future building wings could be sort of "plugged in" along the way, as the need emerged. The central element, to be built sometime in the future, will be a 4,000 seat-Sanctuary, anchoring the two corridors at the corner of the property. I believe we coped well, and the result was enthusiastically embraced by the Church. We remain good friends with the Committee Chairman for the Master Plan.

Figure 15-10: First Baptist Church, Pasadena, Texas, Site Model

Our methods in developing our master plans have evolved over the years, but have always been focused on drawing out of the people of the church their dreams and visions, to lead them to consensus, and to help them find ways to fulfill the missions they believe the Lord has given them. During the combined practice of FOA and O/H, we produced formal master plans for forty-six churches and ten other institutions of various sorts.

One of the earliest master plans we did, which resulted in a later building project for us, was for Two Rivers Baptist Church in Nashville. We learned much of how to collect the data and analyze it in this project. It was a few years before the new building went ahead. We had projected a large educational addition in the first phase, and a later large Sanctuary. This was the first project in which we showed how a circulation loop could be provided, and how beneficial it would be. The 50,000-square-foot educational wing was completed in 1985. Because of changes in church leadership and other conditions beyond our control, we were not asked to design the Sanctuary when it was added later.

In 1988 we were hired to design a substantial addition to First Baptist Church of Hendersonville, Tennessee, near Nashville. The existing site was long and narrow and irregular in general shape. After a few weeks exploring possibilities, a church member's family donated a new 29-acre site, and the church decided to relocate. This prompted the need for a master plan of this new site. We went on to design the entire first phase of the new facility, which includes a 2,000-seat Sanctuary, educational space for 1,750, and a 32,000-square foot Family Life Center, which features a gym, various other recreational facilities, and a 400-seat Fellowship Hall, with kitchen and other support spaces. It includes some 161,000 square feet of enclosed space.

Figure 15-11: First Baptist Church, Hendersonville, Tennessee, Exterior

Figure 15–12: First Baptist Church, Hendersonville, Tennessee, Interior

In 1971 as FOA, we had produced a master plan for First Baptist Church of Athens, my home church. Nothing came of it at that time, but in 1988 we did a new master plan for them, and three years later we began the design of two phases of construction, following that master plan. Together they included a new 880-seat Sanctuary, a Music Suite, a new preschool wing, which could support two additional floors in the future, and various improvements in the older parts of the building complex. The existing building was in a neo-gothic style, and when the Committee saw our rendering of the proposed new work, done in a modern vein but with homage paid to the older forms, I was asked, "Is this the same architectural style as our existing Building?"

I replied, "It's the same family, different generation." That seemed to satisfy everybody.

The Committee Chair for these efforts was Jerry McGivney, who had given me a jump-start in architectural drafting those many years ago by asking me to take over a house-drafting job for him. In the mid-1950s, my father served as Committee Chair for an earlier education addition at FBC Athens.

Figure 15-13: First Baptist Church, Athens, Alabama, Exterior

Figure 15-14: First Baptist Church, Athens, Alabama, Interior

This was not the first project in which we had designed an asymmetrical Sanctuary. Earlier we had done so in two smaller churches, First Baptist, White House, Tennessee, and New Hope Baptist, Hermitage, Tennessee. Partly just to breathe new life into the settings for worship, another motivation for this new departure was to re-examine the appropriate handling of the immersion baptismal pool, or Baptistry as we Baptists prefer to call it. This is a required feature of all Baptist and many other evangelical churches. Traditionally it has been placed on the central axis of the worship space, at the very back, behind the choir loft. In these buildings everything in the space was symmetrically arranged – a central Lord's Supper or Communion Table on the main floor level, in front of a pulpit, which is on a slightly raised platform, and the choir behind that. The pulpit was in the center of the space because it is important that the preaching of the" Word" be seen as *central* to the worship experience. What all this means is that it places the Baptistry in a remote and elevated position in relation to the congregation. In addition, the usual practice was to place the Baptistry behind a kind of window through which the ritual would be viewed, making it even more difficult for the people in the congregation to connect emotionally and spiritually with the event and its participants.

What we have tried to do in all of our new worship spaces having baptistries is to address these concerns and come up with changes in how the elements are arranged in space so that improvements could be made. Consistent with Baptist orthodoxy, we are convinced that the act of baptism should be just as important to those in the pews as to those involved in the act itself, and that by moving the Baptistry over to one side, it could be lowered and brought closer to the people, making it more accessible to the congregation both visually and spiritually. We have not done this in all our new worship spaces, but it was done in four of them, including First Baptist of Athens. What we *have* done in almost all new worship environments is to remove the implied barrier that a "window" surround and its distancing effect makes between the Baptistry and the people, trying instead to design the Baptistry and its setting so that it will be perceived to be in the same major space as the whole room. In very large worship spaces it becomes difficult to have an asymmetrical design, but it is possible to bring the Baptistry into the same room with everything else.

In shifting the Baptistry to one side it then becomes possible, and even easier, to shift the choir loft to the other side. This has the additional benefit of making it easier for the choir members to observe the Baptism, something virtually impossible to do in the old symmetrical arrangement. In so doing, the platform can and usually will be larger than it likely would have been before, providing more flexibility in staging special presentations. A more recent development, which I am quick to say we didn't invent, is to provide an open space behind the Baptistry, visible to the congregation, for family members of the one being baptized to stand in support. We have included this feature in several of our projects, but not in the Athens church.

Another large church is Ridgecrest Baptist in Madison, Mississippi. Beginning with a master plan in 1993, we first designed and built a Family Life Center. In addition, the master plan projected the need for a worship space of 1,600 seats, plus new offices and music ministry facilities. The Family Life Center provided, in its high school size gym, interim space for worship during the longer time required for the larger and more permanent Sanctuary to be designed and built. In connecting the new Sanctuary addition to the existing building, a generous circulation loop was created. This worship space, like most of our larger ones, features Balcony "wings," which sort of sweep down to the main floor on either side of the space, uniting the seating, and, more importantly, making it easy for those in the congregation to respond to the "Invitation," or altar call, which is an integral part of every regularly scheduled worship service in evangelical churches, coming at the end of the sermon. If you've ever attended or watched a Billy Graham Crusade on television, you will recognize this as the same kind of thing, on a smaller scale. This feature was also used in First Baptist, Hendersonville; Hermitage Hills Baptist, Hermitage, Tennessee; and North Boulevard Church of Christ, Murfreesboro, Tennessee.

The most unique feature of Ridgecrest Baptist is probably the 152-foot steeple, which has not only the traditional upward thrust, but also a strong forward thrust as well, signifying the dynamic faith of this congregation. Interestingly, during construction a cell phone company approached the Church, requesting permission to mount an antenna inside the cross at the top of the steeple. A new all-fiberglass cross, provided by the cell phone company, was substituted for the original, and it seems to have worked out to the benefit of both church and the company.

Figure 15-15: Ridgecrest Baptist Church, Madison, Mississippi, Exterior

Figure 15-16: Ridgecrest Baptist Church, Madison, Mississippi, Interior

Most balconies designed and built in the past are accessible only from the front Vestibule, which is discouraging to someone feeling called to respond to an invitation, who might not want to take the long walk down the stairs from the Balcony to the Vestibule, and then down the aisle to the altar; or they might start down and lose heart before arriving there. Even in worship spaces with Balconies but without the "sweeps" we have almost always provided what are often called "response stairs" down from the Balcony within the same room, leading down from the Balcony to the main floor near the altar.

One church with Balcony response stairs and not "sweeps" is First Baptist of Jasper, Alabama. In an earlier chapter I told that I had been born in Jasper. My parents had been members of this church at the time, but neither of these facts had anything to do with O/H being hired to design this building. It came as a result of the Pastor, Dr. Mike Adams, coming to our church, Forest Hills Baptist, to preach a revival, and he and I met there. Some months later he called and asked if I could meet with his Committee. We set this up and had the meeting, and were hired, first to do a master plan, and then to design a new Sanctuary.

The Church in Jasper is situated on a series of rather small city blocks. In addition the land is hilly, steep in places. As was so often the case, we began with a master plan, and finally the Committee and we arrived at the conclusion that the best location for a new Sanctuary, the primary need, was exactly where the existing one then stood. This older building was built in 1949, and was too small and had circulation and access problems, in addition to being costly to operate and maintain. It was demolished, and our new building was erected right back in the same place. However, it was turned around so that the pulpit end is now opposite the end that connects to the remaining parts of the building, making circulation easier and more practical. This church was designed with the traditional symmetrical arrangement, but with the family space behind the Baptistry.

One interesting thing occurred during the design. The existing pipe organ was to be relocated to the new building and refurbished and enlarged. The original organ builder, who claimed that they still had the drawings from the original installation, was contacted for this work. When we sent them copies of the drawings for our new building, they were puzzled, and couldn't seem to make sense of things. It was finally determined that the drawings they had were from an earlier FBC building, built in the 1920s and located across the street, from which the organ they built had been relocated once before to the 1949 building, and they had no record of that move.

Figure 15-17: First Baptist Church, Jasper, Alabama, Exterior

Figure 15-18: First Baptist Church, Jasper, Alabama, Interior

Alabama Boy

A very different project is the "Worship Center Plus" addition at The Donelson Fellowship in Nashville. A Free Will Baptist congregation, this church asked for a multi-purpose facility usable for worship, drama, fellowship meals, and recreation. With a rather tight budget, and limited land, we were able to develop a design that accomplished all these goals by combining uses wherever possible. This includes using the main space for all four of the programmed functions, but also for much of the circulation between support spaces. In addition, to conserve space we devised a platform that folds up into the wall, much like a Murphy bed, to clear the floor for basketball or other sports. When let down the platform projects out into the main space, as needed for worship and drama. An overhead catwalk provides a place to locate theatrical lights, and gives access to many of the house lights, for service to them. There is also a clerestory above, bringing natural light into the space.

In almost all large worship facilities, beginning with First Baptist, Hendersonville, we have designed catwalks above the ceiling to give access to house and theatrical lighting. In recent times, the sound equipment in these churches has required more and more room and prominence of location. We always try to make provision for these elements that will not conflict with, or visually detract from, a comprehensive and coordinated design concept for the space. Just as we try to do with mechanical and electrical elements, we believe it is important for these things to be as "invisible" as possible to the people. We want it to be so that no one is aware of them, just thankful the benefits are there. We don't want anyone to hear the air conditioning system operate, nor to see the light fixtures directly. My personal belief is that a church sanctuary is no place for a chandelier. They are visually detracting, and likely to create glare, making vision difficult.

In our practice we also have designed a few small churches, among them two for Korean congregations, and one for The Salvation Army. This last was unique in that it is for a transient congregation, and features a worship space seating only 125. It has most of the other usual program spaces found in larger churches – offices, classrooms, and a dining hall, plus uniquely, an apartment for visiting clergy. In the exterior design we tried to reflect the military character of The Salvation Army, and in addition clearly show that it is a church, by designing the worship area to make this element very different in form from the rest of the building.

Figure 15-19: Salvation Army Nashville Citadel Corps, Madison, Tennessee, Exterior

Figure 15-20: Salvation Army Nashville Citadel Corps, Madison, Tennessee, Interior

We were called in to meet with the Building Committee at First Baptist, Cookeville, Tennessee and almost didn't even get to talk to them. On the drive over to Cookeville, some 100 miles east of Nashville, for our initial meeting, my car broke down. Ed and I were together and he called the Church on his cell phone and told them what had happened, and offered to just drop out of consideration for the commission. They were very accommodating and agreed to reschedule the interview. We were hired to help them re-examine their entire "plant," or building complex and site, and project future needs and possible solutions; in other words, a master plan, though it wasn't called that. What that project evolved into was a comprehensive renovation of almost every space in the large building complex, including enlarging the Sanctuary without adding any square feet. When the original Sanctuary had been built in the 1960s, provision had been made to "capture" some additional unfinished area at the front of the Sanctuary for whatever use might be needed in the future. Our project pushed the Sanctuary into this area, and added a new, higher roof over it, making the Sanctuary larger, and modernizing it at the same time.

The entire Pulpit/Platform/Choir/Baptistry end of the room is all new. New balcony response stairs were added. On the outside we added a new steeple to an existing all-brick bell tower, and every wall surface of the Sanctuary was changed. The changes to the building, both inside and outside, are not necessarily what everyone might think would be "modernizing." The style of the original building was in a very 1960s modern vein. The Church wanted the building to be more timeless, and what we came up with is what I called "Transitional." It "seems" traditional, but actually is all original in design and details.

The Sanctuary addition for First Baptist of Smyrna, Tennessee, is a different sort of church building. This church is a follower of the "seeker" philosophy, wherein the focus is on the unchurched, or those "seeking" spiritual answers for their lives. This concept was initiated and promoted into a major movement by a large independent church in Illinois, the Willowcreek Community Church. Many large churches, usually independent or nondenominational, have adopted all or some of the ideas of Willowcreek. These include no choir, relying rather on small ensembles and soloists, heavy use of audio-visual technologies, no songbooks or hymnals but projecting the words to songs on large screens, and on drama. The seating is often more akin to movie theater "stadium" seating than to pews, and what we usually call the Platform more closely resembles a theater stage. First Baptist of Smyrna has most of these features, including provision for full stage rigging. It has a capacity of some 1,600, capable of future expansion to about 2,100. It has been an interesting design challenge, and we are sure it will be well received. My associate at O/H and at HFR, Jonathan Whitten, played a major role in the design of this church.

First Baptist of Joelton, located in a suburb of Nashville, presented an interesting site challenge. Though the Church has a reasonably large site in terms of acreage, the street frontage is relatively narrow. In addition, an existing cemetery in the middle of the site had to be integrated into the site development plan in a sensible and gracious way. The program requirements included a new 1,100-seat Sanctuary, plus a few classrooms and a music suite, and all of which had to connect sensibly and efficiently to the circulation system of a rather large existing building complex. In response to these constraints, we placed the new building back in the interior of the site, past the cemetery, linked to the existing with generous corridors, and provided an approach from the street with a sort of tree-lined boulevard, visually drawing people into the center of things, to the front door of the Sanctuary. The Sanctuary itself is turned forty-five degrees from the approach drive axis, but the terminus of the boulevard is a drive-thru canopy with a small steeple, oriented on that axis, visually anchoring the end of the drive. This Sanctuary is asymmetrical, similar to FBC Athens, with all of the Choir risers being removable. Another feature is a video projection rear-screen installation. During non-use times the screen is partially obscured by a pair of rolling panels with cut-outs which form a back-lit cross when in the closed position, and reveal the screen when pulled back.

Almost all of the churches we designed during my entire career have projection screens incorporated into the designs. Most have screens that drop down from a concealed slot in the ceiling. In a couple of the early ones the screens are located in the Platform floor, and are raised by cable and winch systems in the ceilings. However, in recent years the increased use of video projection in worship services has led to another innovation, projecting directly on a fixed screen or in many cases two screens on the front walls. In two of our later churches, FBC, Cookeville and Hermitage Hills BC, we took things a step further by selecting a grille cloth for the organ screens that has certified projection qualities, and having those surfaces double as projection and organ screens. The projectors themselves can be suspended from the overhead, and in the case of Lake Providence Missionary BC, are on retractable supports that can lift them into the ceiling when not needed.

This leads to the last church I want to tell about, Lake Providence Missionary Baptist Church of Nashville, which was completed in early 2003. This building is the home of a large dynamic, and historic Africa American congregation. Moving from a site just two miles away, where they had worshipped for over 140 years, they have built a facility with a Sanctuary seating 3,000 in pews and 300 in the Choir loft, plus offices, education space, support spaces, and a Fellowship Hall for 500. The 37-acre site, terraced to deal with steep slopes, holds parking for over 1,000 cars.

The Lake Providence project has been a true joy for me and my colleagues. It is the second church I have designed for an African American congregation. The people there, beginning with Pastor Bruce Maxwell, mentioned earlier, were so very cooperative and grateful for the things we were able to bring to the project. Many, including Rev. Maxwell and Committee Chair, Jerrold Smith, have become what I consider to be life-long friends. I may never have the opportunity to do work for them again, but what we have experienced together has created a bond that is much more important than any commercial consideration.

Figure 15-21: Lake Providence Missionary Baptist Church,
Nashville, Tennessee, Exterior

Figure 15-22: Lake Providence Missionary Baptist Church,
Nashville, Tennessee, Interior

* * *

One factor which I believe has seriously warped the quality of design in recent years, is the advent of the computer in architectural practice. I will admit that computers have made many of the more routine tasks of the production side of architecture easier and more efficient, but it has conditioned many young people in the field to believe that anything worth doing is better done on a computer. Not only is this patently not true, it has interfered with their mental and professional development by limiting their ability to visualize and explore options as they engage in the very free-roaming kind of activity we call "design." The Architectural Registration Examination (ARE) compounds this by being totally conducted on conducted on computers.

A key and essential trait that all architects should have, in my opinion, is that their thinking patterns should be non-linear, that is, they should be able to look at many aspects of a situation at the same time, and formulate tentative design solutions, that then can be tested and refined. This can be called "intuition," and is akin to "multi-tasking," which all good architects ought to have in abundance. The trouble with computers is that they impose a linear thinking pattern on whatever tasks are done on them, and leave little room for intuition.

Architects must have is the ability to visualize and conceptualize in the third dimension. Some might say that there are computer programs that illustrate things in three dimensions. The flaw in that position is that illustrating them on the computer comes after the conceptualizing of the design has been done. In order to have the digital data in that program needed to construct a three dimensional picture, it is necessary to input it one linear step at a time. This is linear thinking, not non-linear thinking.

With computers one has to take the work one step at a time, in the correct order, from A to B to C, etc. In non-linear thinking the pattern is more like taking A, B, C, etc. all at once, mixing them up in a kind of intellectual stew, keeping the big picture continuously in focus. Linear thinking is like working through a long and complicated math problem, knowing that at the end there is only one "right" answer. Non-linear thinking, on the other hand, is more like exploring, dealing with an entire range of possibilities simultaneously. In linear thinking there can be only one correct answer or outcome. In Architecture there can be many different outcomes. Non-linear thinking frequently leads to a "conclusion," but not to a single "right" answer, and linear thinkers may find this frustrating. On the computer screen only a very small part of the picture can be seen at on time, and that generates tunnel vision, stunted architects, and compromised architecture.

*   *   *

In church buildings the use of the cross is obviously an important consideration – how it is applied and depicted. It seems that much of the time, especially in evangelical churches, not much thought has been given to these concerns. In my practice I have tried to address these things in ways that are theologically appropriate and sound, and where possible, in ways that enhance the impact or effect of seeing a cross on or in a building. The recent film, The Passion of the Christ, has intensely and graphically shown that the cross was a horrible thing. Aside from its spiritual meaning, it was degrading and demeaning to the entire human race, one of the cruelest forms of execution ever devised by the evil minds of mankind. Why then, should it be depicted as a pristine, beautifully rendered object of adoration, as we usually find it?

As we addressed these thoughts in our church designs, we have tried to use the cross in ways that steer people toward a more theologically authentic understanding of the cross and its meaning. These measures have included rendering the cross form itself as a void, defined in outline by something else, or as something crude and rough, or as a form sort of branded into a wall, rather than applied to it. At Lake Providence Missionary Baptist Church, we depicted the cross in a series of unconnected slot windows, expressing the idea of a fractured cross, one that has been shattered by Christ's triumphant sacrifice. I would hope that other church architects would give more thought to the implications of similar design challenges. An expression of a cross rendered at an entirely different scale is a gold cross I designed and had made for Nancy. It features the cross as a void.

* * *

"We are what we repeatedly do. Excellence, then, is not an act, but a habit." *Aristotle*

At Orr/Houk we adopted **Excellence in Architecture** as our motto, and incorporated it into the logo appearing below. The following was addressed to our employees.

Excellence in Architecture is not a style, nor is it merely excellence in architectural design, although that is an essential part of it.

Excellence in Architecture is basically an attitude about what the architect is doing and why it is being done, a mindset focusing on the idea of excellence in the doing, rather than the product. If this can be done then the product will be much more likely to be excellent. It is constantly reminding oneself to do one's best, because that is what one's client deserves. It requires absolute honesty, with oneself as well as everyone else. It requires the total absence of cynicism; because, to surrender to cynicism is to deny the possibility of doing one's best; our motives become tainted, and our loyalties become divided, introducing distracting and harmful stresses into our critical thinking. Finally, it requires the willingness to face challenges and take risks in the quest for excellence.

Ideally, the architecture of excellence we produce should have these characteristics: it should be

Enriching - to the environment and the people whose lives are touched by it, both casual passers by as well as daily users; it should be

Enabling - to those who use it and are otherwise touched by it to do better what they have to do, to reach farther, achieve more; it should be

Extending - beyond the minimum requirements of program or function, to push the limits of what is possible and appropriate; it should be

Exceptional - in every way possible within responsible respect for the Owner's needs, budget, and schedule.

Achieving EXCELLENCE IN ARCHITECTURE means the difference between the EXCEPTIONAL and the ordinary, between the SUPERLATIVE and the merely adequate.

While I confess to falling far short of this lofty goal much of the time in my own practice, I believe that by working to maintain this focus on excellence we cannot help but raise the level of quality of our work, and will occasionally reach that elusive goal of excellent architecture. Just as surely, though, I believe that if we do not, we will never achieve it, and we will be locked into the oppressiveness of mediocrity.

I, for one, do not want to be known for mediocrity; I want to be known for excellence.

*   *   *

While architects hope that our buildings will outlive us, and be seen as our memorials, friends are more important than buildings. And while some of my buildings may last beyond my lifetime as meager reminders of my life, family and friends have blessed me more than have buildings.

16.

TRAVEL

"Strong and content I travel the open road"
                              Walt Whitman

*I*n the chapter titled FLORENCE, I described my typical Saturday morning as a young boy, which included going to the movies to see a double feature, a cartoon and a serial. Among the more memorable films were the Tarzan stories, supposedly set in Africa, although likely shot in California. One serial was "Nyoka of the Jungle," featuring a good-looking girl swinging around on vines and such, like Tarzan did. These, and other things I came across about Africa in my youth sort of emotionally bonded me with Africa early on. I had always wanted to visit Africa, and since those early days I have felt a curious kinship with it that is difficult to understand or explain. As time went on and I became more aware of other places, this fascination has expanded to a wider vision of the world, and a desire to visit as many as possible. When we lived on Meridian Street in Florence our next door neighbors had two children close in age to Johnny and me. They subscribed to the National Geographic, and I spent untold hours at their house looking at copies of it, longing to visit those exotic places.

Travel, mainly international travel, has become a hobby of sorts for Nancy and me, what we do with our free time and discretionary income. Some of our early travel was in the care of the US government (NROTC and the Air Force), and some over the years has been church-sponsored, in other words, mission trips. Most of these, in both categories, have been described elsewhere. In one other case I went to Panama as a part of a team to provide design services to the US Army Corps of Engineers at some of the American facilities in and around the Canal Zone.

Nowadays almost all architecture students are offered the opportunity and are encouraged to take a semester or other term overseas as part of their curriculum. That wasn't available to me, and generally not to many architectural students of my generation. However, the NROTC experience substituted for some of that, and whetted my appetite for more travel. It showed me the benefits of seeing first hand some of what I have learned to call my "A-list" of architectural sites, those every architect should see if at all possible. In our private travel, both in the States and overseas, we have tried to include as many of these as we could.

In 1987, in observance of our thirtieth anniversary, Nancy and I went to Australia and New Zealand. Driving on the left side of the road for the first time was not much of a challenge. Only one time did I forget and start out on the right side. Fortunately no one was coming and I quickly made a correction with no adverse results.

In Australia we visited Melbourne, Canberra, and Sydney, as well as many smaller towns and sites along the way, We saw several botanical gardens, and at least two zoos. One highlight for me was the then still under-construction new Parliament Building in Canberra, designed by an American firm, selected by a design competition.

In New Zealand we started at Auckland and worked our way south, stopping at Rotorua to see the renowned hut sulfur springs, and to enjoy a traditional Maori performance at what was billed as a "Hangi," featuring fierce mock battles, songs, dances, etc. This was accompanied by a typical Maori feast, sort of like a Luau, a buffet with all kinds of indigenous foods. A very enjoyable evening. One of the buildings at Rotorua worth seeing is the Rotorua Bowling Club. It is a very large structure, and in design, in the Late Victorian mode. It is quite impressive.

One of the most pleasant parts of our entire trip was the opportunity to meet new people, like the couple we sat at the same table with in Rotorua, Mark and Jane, from Adelaide, Australia. Meeting new people and making new friends has continued to be among the most delightful benefits of our travel.

At Taupo, a tiny village on a lake shore, we attended services in a small Baptist church. We found it to be an uplifting experience, just enough different from our usual church services at home to be interesting, and still very much alike. The primary difference was that things there were quite informal, compared with our typical experiences in the States.

Before leaving the States I had arranged to give a lecture at the School of Architecture at Victorian University in Wellington. Also, while in Auckland, we had visited briefly with the Dean of the architecture school at Auckland University.

On the South Island we drove our rental car into Christchurch before stopping. The highlight of our stay there was to climb to the top of the steeple of the Cathedral for the views. It was strenuous work, but worth the effort.

We have continued to climb towers and steeples wherever we have found them elsewhere in our travels. These include similar structures in Amsterdam, Rothenburg (Germany), Hamilton (Bermuda), Florence, and Venice (although there we used the elevator). The most unique was at Our Savior Church in Copenhagen, where it is possible to climb all the way to the point of the steeple. The last stretch is an open-air stair spiraling around the spire. When we got to the open stage at the bottom of the spire, I wasn't sure I wanted to go any farther, but Nancy just trudged on higher, and I didn't want to let her show me up, so up we went, all the way to the top. While it is daunting and scary, especially if you are an acrophobe, the views are magnificent, and the climb worth it. A similar experience is hiking up inside the domes of churches like St. Peter's in Rome and St. Paul's in London, and then out into the open-air levels at the highest accessible points.

Our next traveling adventure was two years later when we toured the eastern US, on the outward leg following the Appalachian mountains, stopping at Monticello and Gettysburg, and then back down following a more coastal route. This also took three weeks, and, being the worrier he is, my partner, Ed Houk, was very anxious while I was away. However, he and the firm survived, and we continued to plan similar trips. Among impressive site we saw on this trip are Mount Vernon, the Mark Twain house in Hartford, the Edison Home and labs, Williamsburg, and Old Salem and Biltmore in North Carolina. We skipped New York City. We did, however, spend enough time in Washington to see some of the architecturally important sites we had not seen before, mainly the Vietnam Veterans Memorial, the Air and Space Museum, and the East Wing of the National Gallery.

Our visit to Williamsburg took an unexpected turn. As we drove toward Washington, where we had arranged to stay with my fraternity brother, Ed Moore, and his wife, Helen, our car began to show severe stress, the transmission was slipping, and it got worse the farther we went. We managed to get to their house in Arlington. The next day Ed took me to drop off the car at a place where we the repairs could be done (unfortunately rebuilding the transmission). Ed escorted us into Washington, and showed us around. He did something else, though, which is above the call of duty. While our car repairs were underway, he lent us his second car, a huge barge of a vehicle, a 1970 something Cadillac. Not everyone would do that.

On both of these trips we drove our selves, in rental cars in the Far East, and our own car in the US, and we stayed mostly in bed and breakfast places.

We liked the freedom driving ourselves provided, and in 1993 we undertook the same kind of trip to Europe. Before leaving the States we arranged for rental cars and for our lodging in London, our first stop. After that we just found B & B's along the way wherever we happened to be. That worked out just fine. The only drawback was that we spent a lot of time looking for lodging, and that may have kept us from spending more time sightseeing.

The supreme architectural high point of our time in England was, for me at least, Coventry Cathedral. Designed by Sir Basil Spence to replace the medieval one destroyed in German bombing in WWII, this is one of the most inspiring buildings I have ever visited. With the burned out shell of the original next to it, the new church, in totally modern vernacular, fits the site and serves its architectural purposes perfectly. Other places in England we visited include Stonehenge, Salisbury Cathedral, and, of course, many of the tourist places in London.

We ended the English part of our tour, to take an overnight ferry to Cherbourg, in Portsmouth, where we turned in our rental car, leaving my camera in the car. I had also done the same thing in New Zealand. And on a mission trip to Guatemala in 1982 I left a camera in the New Orleans airport on the way there. I was never able to retrieve any of those cameras, and Nancy never seems to miss an opportunity to remind me of these events.

We arrived in Cherbourg on a national holiday, November first. Before leaving home we had arranged to pick up a rental car there at the dock, but when we arrived, about seven o'clock in the morning, there was no car and no one to contact about it because it was a holiday. The only people in the terminal after the other travelers had left were those manning ticket booths for the two shipping lines using that terminal. I struck up a conversation with one of them, who turned out to be an American expatriate. He knew the owner of the car rental company, and called him for us. We had planned to start our tour that day, driving on to the next stop.

However, we couldn't have the car we had reserved until the next day, so the rental man brought a different car for us to use until the next day, when we would turn it in for the one we had reserved. During that day we drove to St. Mont Michelle, one of our prime A-list sites, and then back to Cherbourg at the end of the day. It all worked out very nicely.

After that we drove through the Loire valley, stopping at Chenanceau, and then up to Chartres, mainly to see the Cathedral. Somehow we got the car on a pedestrian-only street there and had a time getting out of that mess!

After that we worked our way to Paris, where we had phoned ahead to a delightful family-owned hotel on Rue Cler, recommended by Rick Steves' book, Europe Through the Back Door. Although it would be impossible to see everything in Paris in three weeks, much less three days, we tried. Walking, the first day we started at Notre Dame, then Ste. Chapelle, across the street and surrounded by government office buildings. You have to go through a security gate to get in. This is probably my favorite building in Paris. On that day we also visited the Pompidou Center, a large, visually-arresting, ground-breaking modern art museum, featuring an exposed exterior structural skeleton, and stairs and escalators on the outside. It was very controversial at the time it was built. Seeing this building was especially intriguing for me because its design had been determined by a design competition that I had entered. The completed building is nothing like my submittal; it is much better.

We discovered that Parisian restaurants generally don't open till seven o'clock. We like to have our dinner earlier. The solution was a boulangerie (bakery) just a few yards from our hotel, where we could buy sandwiches, quiche and pizza, along with coffee and pastries.

We rode the elevator all the way to the top of the Eiffel Tower, "did" the Louvre, the Arc de Triomphe, and the Musee D'orsay, along with visiting a few other choice Parisian highlights. You really can't do much more in three days. On a second trip to Europe, two years later, we flew through Paris and "collected"a few of the sights we missed that time.

Driving east as we left Paris, we stopped at Ronchamp to see the Corbu (Corbusier) chapel. This is one of the landmark buildings of the last century, and still is as fresh and captivating as when it first appeared. It is revolutionary and daring in its concept and execution.

In Switzerland we toured leisurely through this beautiful country, and spent one night in Montreaux before driving back into France, across the Alps. Before leaving Switzerland though, we had a couple of rather amusing incidents. Driving through a small town, we found that the road we knew we needed to take was barricaded off. It was a Sunday morning and there was almost no one around. We drove around the streets a while and finally came upon a young lady pushing a baby stroller along the side of the street. I stopped, and in my four or so words of French, tried to ask her for directions. She and I struggled back and forth for several minutes, and then in perfect English, she said, "You wouldn't happen to speak English, would you?"

She helped us out, explaining that a birthday street party had been held the night before, and that no one had bothered to remove the barriers that morning. She gave us more detailed directions and we went on our way. The other time we came upon a sign saying, "Panorama," and, thinking it was some sort of sight to see I turned in, only to find that it was a parking garage. To get out I had to have Swiss money, which at that time I had not bothered to obtain. I had to walk several blocks before I found a hotel where I could exchange some money to pay for our unintended parking, and leave.

The remainder of this trip carried us to several places in Provence, visiting primarily Roman ruins, to the walled medieval town of Carcassonne, and into Spain. We had a delightful stay in Barcelona, being impressed most by the Gaudi work, and then spent a couple of days in Madrid before flying home.

Sitting in the Madrid airport waiting to catch the flight back to the States, we made out a list of places in Europe we had not seen on this trip. Two years later we took a tour with Rick Steves company, visiting all but one of those places. The one exception was Copenhagen, which I had visited on my 1951 NROTC cruise, and wanted to see again, with Nancy. In 2003 we spent a week there on our own.

On our 1995 trip we started in Haarlem, near Amsterdam, going through Holland, the Rhine Valley and other German sites, into Austria, winding our way through Italy, Switzerland and France. All of the stops were enjoyable and sometimes thrilling. Among the most memorable are a boat ride down the Rhine, flying down a luge chute in the summertime on a wheeled sled, seeing Venice, Sienna and Florence for the first time and Rome again. Also, Cinque Terra, and Bellagio on Lake Como, staying in a tiny hotel in the Alps, reachable only by cable car, and trying to "do" the rest of the Paris sights we missed two years earlier, in three days. It couldn't be done, but we enjoyed the effort.

In 1997 we toured the ancient and a few modern sights in Egypt, lodging and traveling mostly on one of the large Nile River boats, seeing temples, pyramids, the Sphnix, and many others that had been the objects of intense study in my architectural history courses in College. One in particular is Queen Hatshepsut's Tomb. Bruce Knodel and I built a model of this in an architectural history class at Auburn. In Egypt the weather is dry, with only about two inches of rain a year, usually coming in one month, January. It is also hot, but, being dry, we didn't suffer too much.

Architectural highlights for me in Egypt include Abu Simbel, and a surprise – the Cheops Boat Museum, where a 120 foot long boat ,dating from about 1200 BC, has been reassembled and housed in a new building built exclusively for its display.

Finally, at the pyramids we had a camel ride. Nancy and I rode the same beast, and for me it was not all that great. I wore shorts and the saddle blanket was made of something close kin to steel wool. The insides of my thighs were abraded almost to the point of drawing blood, or at least it felt like it.

Since then, beginning in 1999, we have traveled several times with Overseas Adventure Travel, a tour company specializing in trips to unusual places, limiting the size of the the groups to a maximum of sixteen, offering "adventurous" experiences. On these trips we have been to such different places as Tanzania, Peru, Ecuador, the Galapogos, Morocco, plus in 2003 to Thailand, Cambodia, Burma, Japan, and unofficially one other country we aren't allowed into. On many of these trips we have traveled with some of the same adventurers, and have become fast friends with them. Angkor Wat in Cambodia, was the primary drawing card for me for that trip. Seeing it is a once-in-a-lifetime experience, on a par with Machu Picchu in Peru.

In 2001 we traveled to Morocco, also with OAT, with some of the same friends we met in Peru two years before. Like all of our overseas trips, it was delightful. However, the return trip home wasn't entirely joyful. We left Marrakech on an in-country flight to

Casablanca, where we would catch our overseas flight to New York. We were rushed, and things were hectic at the check-in counter. We didn't realize till later that the clerk at Marrakech had failed to give us our luggage claim checks. We arrived at JFK on a Saturday. Everyone's bags arrived in New York with the plane, except ours. We went looking for the appropriate people with whom to file a claim for lost luggage. The New York Royal Moroc Airlines folks told us to go on home on our scheduled flight on Delta, and file a claim here in Nashville when we got home. We did just that, and were told here to call Royal Moroc on the next Monday. We did that, too, and found that their office was closed that day. We had lost luggage before, but this was the most distressing we had experienced thus far. Finally, on Monday night about six we got a call from the local Delta office, telling us that they had our bags and would deliver them to our home. They arrived in about thirty minutes, looking beaten, but intact. From the routing tags on the bags we discovered that they had traveled to Marseille and Paris before finding their way home to us.

Continuing, in the fall of 2005 we went to Japan with OAT and some of our traveling buddies. We expect to keep on traveling as long as the Lord gives us the health and strength for it.

Our next trip is planned for Libya, where Nancy and I spent the first months of our marriage. While there we'll try to find the little

house we called home, and revisit some of the other places that were familiar to us during that time.

Travel is probably the main thing Nancy and I do instead of play golf or engage in any other such time-consuming hobby. We get to see interesting places, meet new friends, have memorable adventures and I get to make travel sketches. We have ridden camels and elephants, and in hot air balloons, slept in tents and similar primitive lodgings in the Serengeti, the Amazon, and the Sahara, using equally primitive toilet and shower facilities. And have seen close up wild animals and gorgeous but sometimes crumbling temples among many, many other thrilling sights. Getting lost, losing cameras, and just meeting the unexpected are all part of the adventure, the fun, and we love it.

Figure 16-6: Nancy and Frank, Tanzania, 1999

17.

THE LAST WORD

"Passion is like an artesian well – when tapped, it brings life and energy to even the most barren desert. Passion, like attitude, is contagious and is essential for a project to succeed. Life is an adventure, not a worry, and if you want to pursue a dream, stumbling blocks must become stepping stones. Passion is a powerful thing and when directed properly it can help bring visions to reality."

Photographer Ken Duncan
in his book AMERICA WIDE, 2001

I believe that the kind of passion described above is essential to being an architect, and to making authentic architecture. In our practice Ed and I would sometimes remark to each other that such and such employee just didn't have any "fire in the belly," meaning he (or she) was just coasting along, seemingly having no passion. I have been known to describe this condition as having one's mind in "cruise control." This can trickle down (or up) to the process of conceptualizing a design, producing humdrum designs, just because that was easier to do that than to spend the time and intellectual energy that every commission deserves. This is "Hack" architecture.

At the 1985 convention of the Tennessee Society of Architects I spoke up in a forum, attended by most who had come to the convention, and made a statement to the effect that eighty percent of architects were hacks. Of course this did not sit too well with my colleagues. As is too often the case I was impulsive, intemperate, and imprecise in my speech. I had intended this accusation to apply to only the eighty percent of Tennessee architects who weren't at the convention, but also I meant to say and should have said that many architects are hacks eighty percent of the time. I believe this statement can be defended; you only have to look around and see the abysmal quality or lack thereof in building design being produced today to find evidence of this. This is especially appalling to me because of my concentration in church design. New church buildings in my opinion can be placed in three categories - very good, so-so, and terrible. The so-so seem to predominate and the terrible show up all too often. The very good unfortunately are rare.

I believe that this also applies to other building types, but churches present opportunities for more creativity than many other types, and I find it disheartening that so many church buildings are so poor in vision and sensitivity to their purposes. It seems to be so easy to just copy and adapt what has been designed before for some other congregation. One reason for this is the ascendance of the church design/build contractor. The design/build movement in construction has many supporters, and it may be appropriate for some building types, however, to my mind it is particularly ill suited to application in church buildings. It may seem beneficial for the church to have a single source provider, but what is not admitted, if known at all, is that the design/build contractor is motivated primarily by profit, and one of the simplest ways to maximize profit is to skimp on design, and quality of materials and construction standards. An easy way to do that is to reuse and adapt a design from an earlier project.

Churches too often are not led by their architects or contractors to give proper consideration to the long-range impacts of their decisions, or to the visual statement the building makes to the public and their own people about what is the nature and character of the church as an institution. If the experience, insight, and vision of a sensitive and innovative architect are not available to the church, these concerns likely will not be addressed. It is not in the design/build contractor's best interest to spend time on these things. Too often churches settle for "good enough," when it would seem that honoring God would call for a higher standard.

The opposite of the "hack" architect is the "star." This is one who has attracted so much publicity that his every commission is automatically heralded in the media as the next great new thing. Often it is not new at all. One lingering one-liner among architects is, "He hasn't designed twenty buildings; he has just designed one building twenty times." Of course there are architects worthy of the star designation. They have pioneered new directions that have benefited the whole profession and society. However, there are also many who have been touted and elevated to "Pseudo-star" status, whose primary achievement is self-promotion, being more concerned with status and image than with serving others. These we don't need, and fortunately they don't seem to hang around in the public eye very long.

One of the most disturbing things in architecture is the penchant of some architects to take the resources of the great variety of products we have today, and the computer-assisted drafting and other technical aids available today, and try to use every possible design device and as many different materials on every building they design. They show no restraint, no critical thinking about what the building should really be. Those buildings end up looking like a crude, ungraceful collection of disparate forms. My attitude toward this is to remember that, just because it is possible to do something, that is no justification for doing it.

*   *   *

I seem to have genetic flaw that keeps me from wanting to do something that someone else has done before. If I think it is not an original idea, I can't drum up much enthusiasm for it. Maybe that's why I never could finish a model airplane kit when I was a boy. When I began to make my travel sketches, and we used them on our office Christmas cards, Ed tried to get me to make sketches of Nashville buildings for our Christmas Cards because others had done that, and because they might be marketable. Except for one time, I just couldn't make myself do it. Ed also urged me from time to time to do conceptual design sketches for speculative projects, observing that other architects did this, and received commissions afterward. I did try that a few times, but it never seemed to work out for us. That was probably because of my conviction that to properly design something you have to dig into it to a much deeper depth that a simple conceptual sketch allowed. When I proposed the idea for the book, <u>Notable Nashville Architecture</u>, to the local AIA chapter board, I was asked if I knew of any other city where this kind of thing had been done. Of course I didn't, and if I had I wouldn't even think of suggesting it for Nashville. I suppose that the foundational reason for this is my deeply held belief that my role in life is to do original things, in architecture or in any other realm I find myself involved in. I just can't bring myself to be a copycat, even if that label can be found only in my own mind. Maybe this book is an exception. I am sure that every possible variation of form of memoir has already been attempted. Is the approach I have taken here different enough to not violate my obsession with being original? I hope so. This obsession also may make me look like an absolute twit; I hope not, but that's someone else's call.

*   *   *

Appearing in the Spring 2003 issue of Faith and Form, *the journal of the Interfaith Forum on Religious Art and Architecture (IFRAA), this item was written in response to a discussion of Sacred Space in an earlier issue.*

My forty years of practice has been dominated by the design of churches. Many times something has caused me to ponder the term, "Sacred Space," but I have never been able to determine or settle on what for me that means or ought to mean.

I can agree that there are sacred *places,* and that some may be *spaces*; but the fact that they are spaces seems to me to be secondary to the quality of sacredness imposed by something transcendental that has happened there. Significant examples include the World Trade Center site, perhaps some or all of the Nazi death camps, and sites of natural disasters such as floods, tornados, or earthquakes.

World Trade Center site, perhaps some or all of the Nazi death camps, and sites of natural disasters such as floods, tornados, or earthquakes.

I have visited many of the world's A List of religious buildings, defined as those designed and erected for religious purposes. Most, at least among those in Europe where many are found, are more like museums than living spiritual institutions. There are several I would call excellent, but for the most part, that is because of their architecture rather than any spiritual experience when we visit them. Indeed, one of my favorites among these is now a museum, the Hagia Sophia in Istanbul. Having been erected as a magnificent church, and converted to a mosque when the Ottoman Turks took over the

I have visited many of the world's A List of religious buildings, defined as those designed and erected for religious purposes. Most, at least among those in Europe where many are found, are more like museums than living spiritual institutions. There are several I would call excellent, but for the most part, that is because of their architecture rather than any spiritual experience when we visit them. Indeed, one of my favorites among these is now a museum, the Hagia Sophia in Istanbul. Having been erected as a magnificent church, and converted to a mosque when the Ottoman Turks took over the country, it eventually became a museum when Turkey became a secular state. It is a

spectacular space and as astounding structural achievement for its time, and while it literally thrills me as architecture, for me it does not meet the criteria for sacred space.

Probably the most moving spiritual/architectural experience I have had was a visit to the Protestant Chapel at Dachau. I confess that I cried. The Jewish and Catholic Chapels may be stirring architecturally but they failed to move me in any spiritual way. This structure, and I hesitate to call it a building for it is unenclosed, brought me the closest I have ever been to acknowledging the existence of a sacred space. However, the reason for this is not because of what the Chapel is for itself; it is only so as a result of what happened at this site before the Chapel was built. If this Chapel were found anywhere else it would only be an architecturally interesting artifact, with questionable spiritual qualities.

Perhaps some natural sites could qualify as sacred, if one is moved by them to ponder the power, majesty, and glory of God as He has expressed His creation. The Grand Canyon, the great natural waterfalls, the stunning vistas found in the Alps, the Rockies, and other mountain ranges, particularly moving sunrises and sunsets, the sea in all its expressions, and even storms can be seen in this way, and should be. However, the sacredness we feel in these settings is because of what God has done, not man.

This leads me to the conclusion that we cannot create sacred space or spaces. Such places become sacred only because of what God does in those places. For us as designers to assume that we can create sacred space strikes me as both futile and arrogant. Just because we may call a space sacred does not make it so. Only God can do that. We can through our gifts and skills and the participation of our clients perhaps create spaces which lift the emotional spirits of those who use them, may try to remove or avoid intrusions which might detract from a spiritual experience, and hope to enhance the likelihood that spiritual connections may be made there, but that's about as far as we can go. My belief is that the sacredness of any space, no matter who designs it, only becomes sacred when God makes it so, not when man tries to do so.

*   *   *

Remarks made at the dedication of the new building for the Lake Providence Missionary Baptist Church, *February 9, 2003*

It is truly a heart-warming honor to be here with you today. The Lord has blessed all of us, me as much as anyone, because He has made it possible for me to use the gifts He gave me in this way.

I want to talk a little about gifts. In Matthew 25, Jesus tells the parable of the talents. The word "talents" was probably used here as a stand-in for money, but I don't believe it is a theological stretch to give it a more literal meaning – that being the gifts or aptitudes He gives each of us.

The Lord gives each of us gifts – to some music, to some managerial abilities, to some abilities in the visual arts, to some teaching, and perhaps to some medicine or other healthcare work. Your gifts do not have to be defined by your vocation. An example of this kind is the gift of hospitality, or basic kindness. We all probably know someone who is always so positive and life-affirming that we are lifted up and cheered just by being around them.

If you are between the ages of 13 and 18, please stand up. You are at an age where you will still have many life choices before you. You are mature enough, or ought to be, to begin to see the possibilities of life and to recognize how serious your choices can be.

As a Christian just beginning on the journey of life, your responsibility right now is to decide to discover the gifts God has given you if you haven't already done so, to nurture and develop those gifts, and allow God to use you and His gifts to you for His purposes.

Please sit down.

God gifted me with the abilities needed to design structures like this. It is immeasurably gratifying and fulfilling. There are likely several among you to whom He has given the same kinds of gifts, and to some other kinds of gifts, perhaps some the gifts of praising Him in music, and perhaps to some the gift of proclaiming His word in preaching. Whatever your gifts are, use them to the fullest. If your gift is carpentry, for example, be the best, God-praising carpenter you can be.

Don't be hesitant and fearful like the third servant, taking the "safe" but unproductive way. Be like the first and second servants, holding nothing back, risking it all for God.

And it wouldn't surprise me if one day we will see a building as impressive as this or even more so designed by one of you.

Find your gifts. Dedicate them to the Lord and He will wear you out with the work He has planned for you. God bless every one of you.

*   *   *

Those who might be interested in such things probably have noticed that I have not said much here about architectural philosophy. I don't think I have said anything at all about it directly. If my work and attitudes expressed here and in my buildings lead anyone to place a style label on me, they might say that I am a Postmodernist who doesn't know it. That's really just bunk, because no one seems to be able to agree on just what that term means. I really don't want to carry a label of any kind. I don't want to be put into a box that someone else has defined. To me, such labels are harmful in that they put limits on us, when what is truly important is to be open-minded, shunning limits, always exploring new possibilities. I don't mind being called a Husband, a Father, a Christian, a Baptist or an Architect; these are roles I have chosen for myself. What I do mind is having someone else making those choices for me. In addition to the discussion of Excellence in Architecture in the previous chapter, the following gives perhaps the most cogent expression of architectural philosophy I care to have on record.

*   *   *

In 1985 I wrote the following for our staff at Orr/Houk:

What architecture is:

1. Constructed enclosure of space for the uplifting, enhancing, enriching, and enabling of mankind in his activities, work, play, and meditation.
2. Timeless.

What architecture is not:

1. Constructed enclosure of space for the sole purpose of enclosing space.
3. Driven by fashion.

What architecture does:

1. Provides mankind with memorable places, giving him not only immediate pleasure or delight, but also a vision of potential for perpetual human enrichment.

2. Keeps out the weather, provides a controlled temperature and humidity, and functions well in its enabling and enhancement of the human activity it has been designed to house.

Firmness, Commodity, and Delight – if it doesn't have all three, it ain't architecture, its just shelter.
I am an *architect*, not a *sheltertech*..

*   *   *

To wrap up I would like to share a definition I have come to believe is appropriate for the kind of architect the world needs more than either stars or hacks. This is the "Servant Architect," one who respects the concerns and values of society, who attempts to improve his world and community as he has opportunity to do so, and one who works in partnership with his clients to discover what they truly need, even if they do not realize it at first, help them achieve it, bringing to them and the world something more, something that might be called "a little magic." For if we cannot bring that magic to our tasks, then we fall into the hack category. And if we concentrate on originality to the exclusion of other considerations we are likely to think of ourselves as stars, caring more about our own needs than those of the clients. The Servant Architect has a humble opinion of himself, and an intellectually balanced view of what he is to be about.

Figure 17-1: Caricature of Frank, by Dani Aguila, 2005

APPENDIX I
Selected Projects

With Edwin A. Keeble Associates, Inc.
(1962-1970, exact dates unknown)

FIRST UNITED METHODIST CHURCH
    Athens, Alabama
    Sanctuary remodeling

JUDSON BAPTIST CHURCH
    Nashville, Tennessee
    Master Plan and Relocation

FIRST CHRISTIAN CHURCH
    Glasgow, Kentucky
    Master Plan and Relocation

IMMANUEL BAPTIST CHURCH
    Nashville, Tennessee
    New Sanctuary and Fellowship Hall

FIRST BAPTIST CHURCH
    Nashville, Tennessee
    New Sanctuary, Pastor's Offices, Education and Fellowship Hall

SPARTA CHURCH OF CHRIST
    Sparta, Tennessee
    New Auditorium

THE UNIVERSITY OF THE SOUTH
   Sewanee, Tennessee
   McCready Hall - New Residence Building
   Cravens Hall – New Dining/Assembly Building
   Hamilton Hall – New Classroom and Administration Building

MONTEAGLE ASSEMBLY
   Monteagle, Tennessee
   Dining Hall

ATHENS COLLEGE
   Athens, Alabama
   New Gymnasium
   Conversion of an Antebellum House to Faculty Apartments

CUMBERLAND COLLEGE
   Lebanon, Tennessee
   New Student Center
   New Dormitory

H. G. HILL ELEMENTARY SCHOOL
   Nashville, Tennessee
   New K – 6 Elementary School

(Plus several residences and other projects)

Frank Orr Architects
   (1970 –1976, including certain carry-overs to Orr/Houk)

W. T. GRANT STORE
   Cookeville, Tennessee
   1970 – New Department Store

FIRST BAPTIST CHURCH
   Cullman. Alabama
   1971 – Exterior and Interior Renovation

OLD ORCHARD SHOPPING CENTER
    Henderson, Kentucky
    1971 -New Shopping Center

BUNTIN ADVERTISING OFFICE BUILDING
    Nashville, Tennessee
    1972 – Small Office Building

FIFTEENTH AVENUE BAPTIST CHURCH
    Nashville, Tennessee
    1972 – New Gym/Fellowship Hall Addition

BELMONT MANSION
    Nashville, Tennessee
    1972-1974 – Historic Renovations

SMYRNA NURSING HOME
    Smyrna, Tennessee
    1973 – 50-Bed Nursing Home

RIDGECREST BAPTIST CONFERENCE CENTER
    Ridgecrest, North Carolina
    1973 – Lodging in Three New Buildings

THE SOUTHERN BAPTIST SUNDAY SCHOOL BOARD
    Nashville, Tennessee
    1974 – 1997 – Multiple Projects in their Headquarters Building

AMERICAN BAPTIST THEOLOGICAL SEMINARY
    Nashville, Tennessee
    1974 – Master Plan

CLIFFTOPS
    Monteagle, Tennessee
    1974 – Master Plan of an 1885-Acre site for a Second Home Development

JOE L. EVINS APPALACHIAN CENTER FOR CRAFTS
DeKalb County, Tennessee
1974 – New multi-building College-level Institution for the Study and Preservation of Crafts; in Joint Venture with Cain-Schlott Architects

WOODMONT BAPTIST CHURCH
Nashville, Tennessee
1975 – Restoration of the Burned Chapel

BAPTIST BOOK STORES
Fourteen Sites, Various locations
1975 –1980 – New and remodeled Religious Book Stores

FARMERS BANK AND TRUST
Winchester, Tennessee
1976 - Renovation of an 1899 Building and a Large New Addition,
With Edwin Keeble as the Design Consultant

Orr/Houk and Associates, Architects, Inc.
(1976-2001)

TWO RIVERS BAPTIST CHURCH
Nashville, Tennessee
1977 – Master Plan
1983 – New 50,000 Square Foot Educational Building

GENESCO, INC.
Almost Fifty Stores, Various Sites
1978-1986 – Shoe Stores

SIDCO DRIVE OFFICE/WAREHOUSE DEVELOPMENT
Nashville, Tennessee
1979 – Distribution Center

FIRST BAPTIST CHURCH
   White House, Tennessee
   1980 – Church Relocation

PERRY MEMORIAL HOSPITAL
   Linden, Tennessee
   1980 – New 44-Bed Hospital

WHITWELL MEDICAL CENTER
   Whitwell, Tennessee
   1982 – New 40-Bed Hospital

CUMBERLAND HALL PSYCHIATRIC HOSPITAL
   Nashville, Tennessee
   1984-1986 – Several Additions and Renovations at an Existing Facility

MERIT MUSIC BUILDING
   Nashville, Tennessee
   1984 – New Office Building Featuring the First Installation of Four-sided Structural Glazing in the Eastern US

IMMANUEL BAPTIST CHURCH
   Nashville, Tennessee
   1986 – New Administration Wing

SHADOWBLUFF APARTMENTS
   Nashville, Tennessee
   1984 – A 212-Unit Apartment Development

TENNESSEE BAPTIST CHILDRENS HOMES, INC.
   Chattanooga and Nashville, Tennessee
   1985 – An Activities Building, Chattanooga
   A Headmaster's Residence, Nashville
   1995 – New Headquarters Building, Nashville

DICKENSON COUNTY MEDICAL CENTER
    Clintwood, Virginia
    1985 – A new 40-Bed Hospital

HERMITAGE HILLS BAPTIST CHURCH
    Hermitage, Tennessee
    1985 – Master Plan and Educational and Music Additions
    2000 – Third Floor Addition to 1985 Educational Addition
    2003 – New 2400-seat Sanctuary, Education and Administrative Addition
    (Completed at Hart Freeland Roberts, Inc.)

SOUTHOAKS
    Nashville, Tennessee
    1985 – Office/Warehouse Distribution Center

VANDERBILT UNIVERSITY MEDICAL CENTER
    Nashville, Tennessee
    1985-2001 – 148 Separate Projects, Mostly Renovations, Mostly Research Labs

PARKWAY BAPTIST CHURCH
    Goodlettsville, Tennessee
    1987 – Master Plan and Additions and Renovations

NEW HOPE BAPTIST CHURCH
    Hermitage, Tennessee
    1987 – Master Plan and 720-seat Sanctuary, Office and Music Addition

FIRST BAPTIST CHURCH
    Athens, Alabama
    1988 – Master Plan
    1991 – 880-seat Sanctuary, Music Suite and Education Additions, Various
    Renovations in the Existing Building

FIRST BAPTIST CHURCH
   Hendersonville, Tennessee
   1988 – Master Plan and Relocation, with 2000-seat Sanctuary, plus Education
   Space, Administrative Offices and a Family Life Center; Parking for 1000+ Cars

HARPETH VALLEY ELEMENTARY SCHOOL
   Nashville, Tennessee
   1988 – Replacement K-4 Elementary School

RIDGECREST BAPTIST CHURCH
   Madison, Mississippi
   1993 – Master Plan and Family Life Center
   1994 – New 1600-seat Sanctuary, Administrative Offices and Music Addition

FIRST BAPTIST CHURCH
   Lenoir City, Tennessee
   1993 – Conversion of an Existing Industrial Building into Church Facilities

BETHEL WORLD OUTREACH CENTER
   Nashville, Tennessee
   1993 – Master Plan
   1996 – Education and Recreation Addition, and Various Renovations

NORTH BOULEVARD CHURCH OF CHRIST
   Murfreesboro, Tennessee
   1994 – Relocation of All Facilities, including a 1200-seat Auditorium

FIRST BAPTIST CHURCH
   Dickson, Tennessee
   1991 - Master Plan of an Existing Site
   1994 – Master Plan and Relocation to a New 83-Acre Site

FIRST BAPTIST CHURCH
　　Pasadena, Texas
　　1994 – Master Plan

FOREST HILLS BAPTIST CHURCH
　　Nashville, Tennessee
　　1995 – Master Plan
　　1996 - 53,000 Square Foot Education, Fellowship Hall and Family Life Center Addition
　　2003 – New Master Plan (Completed by Hart Freeland Roberts, Inc.)

FIRST BAPTIST CHURCH
　　Jasper, Alabama
　　1995 – Master Plan
　　1996 – New 960-Seat Sanctuary Addition and Various Renovations

THE DONELSON FELLOWSHIP
　　Donelson, Tennessee
　　1995 – New Multi-purpose Facility Addition

I-440 BUSINESS CENTER
　　Nashville, Tennessee
　　1995 – Office/Warehouse Distribution Center

JUDSON BAPTIST CHURCH
　　Nashville, Tennessee
　　1996 – Renovation of the Existing Sanctuary
　　1999 – Master Plan

THE SALVATION ARMY
　　Madison, Tennessee
　　1996 – New Citadel Corps Facility

FIRST BAPTIST CHURCH
　　Joelton, Tennessee
　　1997 – New 1100-Seat Sanctuary, Education and Music Addition

CARSON SPRINGS BAPTIST CONFERENCE CENTER
Newport, Tennessee
1997 – New Lodge, Conference and Dining Facility

LINDEN VALLEY BAPTIST CONFERENCE CENTER
Linden, Tennessee
1997 – New lodge and Conference Facility

LAKE PROVIDENCE MISSIONARY BAPTIST CHURCH
Nashville, Tennessee
1998 – Various Studies and Site Evaluations
1999 – Master Plan, and New facilities, Including a New 3300-Seat Sanctuary, Education, Administrative Offices and Fellowship Dining Facilities, Parking for over 1000 Cars on a 37-Acre Site
(Construction Completed at Hart Freeland Roberts, Inc.)

THE BLESSED BAPTIST CHURCH
Nashville, Tennessee
1998 – New Facilities for a Korean American Congregation

HICKMAN ELEMENTARY SCHOOL
Nashville. Tennessee
1998 – Replacement K-4 Elementary School

HENRY C. MAXWELL ELEMENTARY SCHOOL
Nashville, Tennessee
1999 – New K-4 Elementary School
(Construction Completed at Hart Freeland Roberts, Inc.)

FIRST BAPTIST CHURCH
Cookeville, Tennessee
2003 – Master Plan, Expanded Sanctuary and General Renovations
(Construction Completed at Hart Freeland Roberts, Inc.)

FIRST BAPTIST CHURCH
Cookeville, Tennessee
2003 – New Sanctuary
(Design and Construction Completed at Hart Freeland Roberts, Inc.)

APPENDIX II

*F*rank's "A List" of architectural sites every architect and lover of architecture ought to see, in no particular order of importance. The criteria for these is that I have personally visited them, and they are in my opinion exceptional. Excluded are natural wonders such as the Grand Canyon, and many other architectural sites of worth that I haven't yet been able to see.

AUSTRALIA:
    Sydney Opera House,
    Sydney Harbor Bridge,
    Sydney

BRAZIL:
    The Christ Statue,
    Rio de Janario

CAMBODIA:
    Angkor Wat

DENMARK:
    Tivoli Gardens,
    The Royal Library,
    Fredericksborg Slot
    Copenhagen
    Brede Open Air Museum
    Lyngby
    Kronborg Castle
    Helsignor

EGYPT:
    Luxor,
    Karnak,
    The Giza Pyramids,
    The Sphnix,
    The Valley of the Kings,
    Queen Hatshepsut's Temple,
    Edfu Temple, Abu Simbel,
    Philae Temple,
    The Nile Valley
    The Old City,
    The Bazaar,
    The Mosque of Mohammed Ali
    Cairo

ENGLAND:
    St. Paul's Cathedral,
    Westminster Abbey,
    London
    Coventry Cathedral,
    Coventry
    Stonehenge,
    Stonehenge
    Salisbury Cathedral,
    Salisbury

FRANCE:
    Le Mont St. Michelle,
    Normandy
    Chenonceaux Chateau,
    Loire Valley
    Chartres Cathedral,
    Chartres
    Notre Dame,
    Ste. Chappelle,
    Sacre Coeur,
    Eiffel Tower,

Arc de Triomphe,
Pompideau Center,
Grande Arche at La Defense,
Paris
Chappelle du Haute,
Ronchamp
The Roman Ruins,
Arles and Nimes
Maison Carree,
Carree d'Art,
Nimes
Carcassonne,
Carcassonne

GERMANY;
Rothenburg,
Rothen burg
Neu Schwanstein,
Bavaria

HOLLAND:
Rijkmuseum,
The Van Gogh Museum,
Amsterdam

ITALY:
St. Peter's Basilica and Square,
The Roman Coliseum,
The Roman Forum,
Piazza Navona,
The Pantheon,
Trevi Fountain,
The Campidoglio,
Rome
The Cathedral,
The Baptistry,
The Ponte Vecchio,

Santa Croce,
Florence
The Campo,
The Cathedral,
Sienna
Vernazza,
The Cinque Terra
St. Mark's Cathedral, Square, and Tower,
Rialto Bridge,
Venice

LIBYA:
Leptis Magna
Sabratha

MOROCCO:
Hassan II Mosque,
The Chellah,
Hassan Tower,
Rabat
Volubilis,
Morocco
The Medina,
Fez
The Casbah
Ben haddou
The Medina,
Al Koutoubia Mosque,
Djemaa El Fna,
Marrakech

PERU:
Machu Picchu,
Cusco,

PORTUGAL:
    St. George Castle,
    Monastery of Jeronimos,
    Belem Tower,
    Explorer's Monument,
    Lisbon
    Sintra,

SPAIN:
    Sagrada Familia Cathedral,
    Barcelona
    The Prado,
    Madrid

TURKEY:
    Hagia Sofia,
    Istanbul

UNITED STATES:
    Monticello
    Virginia
    Mount Vernon,
    Virginia
    Williamsburg,
    Virginia
    Air and Space Museum,
    East Wing, The National Galley,
    Washington, DC
    Old Salem, Winston Salem,
    North Carolina
    Biltmore House,
    Asheville, North Carolina
    Mark Twain Home,
    Hartford, Connecticut
    Trinity Church,
    Boston
    Thomas Edison Home, "Glenmont,"

West Orange, New Jersey
Unity Temple,
Chicago
Frank Lloyd Wright Houses and Studio,
Chicago and Environs
The Chapel at MIT,
Cambridge
St. Mary's Cathedral,
San Francisco
San Simeon,
California
The Wallace House,
Athens, Alabama
The Hermitage,
Nashville

INDEX

Abu Simbel, Egypt, ... 212

AIA College of Fellows, ... 175

AIA Mid-Tennessee, ... 160

AIA Research Corporation, ... 155

A-List of Architectural Sites, ... 204

Alabama Agricultural
    Extension Service, ... 24

Alabama Music Hall of Fame, ... 51

Allen, Mary Belle, ... 23

Africa, ... 203

The Amazon River, Peru, ... 214

American Baptist
    Theological Seminary,
    Nashville, Tennessee, ... 227

American Institute of
    Architects, AIA, ... 149

AMERICA WIDE, ... 215

Amsterdam, Holland, ... 44, 205

Anderson, Robert, ... 120

Angkor Wat, Cambodia, ... 212

Aguila, Dani, ... 224

Antwerp, Belgium, ... 84

The Aquila, ... 58

Architectural Philosophy, ... 222

Architectural Registration
    Examination, (ARE), ... 157

"Architecture is Frozen Music," 53

Aristotle, ... 199

Askew, Garry, ... 44

Athens, Alabama, ... 55

Athens, Greece, ... xi, 112

Athens High School,
    Athens, Alabama, ... 66

Athens College, Athens
    State College, Athens,
    Alabama, ... 144, 226

Auburn University, Alabama, ... 22, 46

Australia, ... 204

Baptist Book Stores, Various Locations, ...154, 228

Baptist Pavilion, 1982 World's Fair, Knoxville, Tennessee, ...176

Baptist Training Union, BTU, ...40

Baptistry, ...185

Barcelona, Spain, ...210

Beam, Kenny, ...44

Beasley Bailey Poultry Company, ...64

Belmont College and University, ...41

Belmont Mansion, Nashville, Tennessee, ...176, 227

Bethel World Outreach Center, Nashville, Tennessee, ...231

Bianculli, Mario, ...149

Birmingham Southern College, ...107

Biltmore House, Asheville, North Carolina, ...206

The Blessed Baptist Church, Nashville, Tennessee, ...233

Brazil, ...45

Brazzi, Rosanno, ...101

Brothers, Russell, ...154

Brown Engineering, Huntsville, Alabama, ...117

Brussels, Belgium, ...84

Buntin Advertising Building, Nashville, Tennessee, ...227

Burma, ...212

Byrd, Davis, ...131

Cain-Schlott, Architects, ...172

Cambodia, ...212

Campbell, Billy, ...50

Canada, ...45

Carcassonne, France, ...210

Carson Springs Baptist Conference Center, Newport, Tennessee, ...170, 233

Casablanca, Morocco, ... xi, 44

Chambers, George, ...26

Chappelle du Haute, Ronchamp, France, ...209

"Charrette," 161

Chartres Cathedral, France, ...208

Chattanooga, Tennessee, ...132

Chenonceaux Chateau, France, ...208

Cherbourg, France, ...207

Chess Pie, ...71

Chewacla State Park,
    Auburn, Alabama, ...91

Churchill, Winston, ...165

Church of Christ,
    Sparta, Tennessee, ...141

Clifftops,
    Monteagle, Tennessee, ...159

Christian Testimony, ...46

The Cross, ...198

Church Design, ...179, 183, 191, 198

The Cinque Terra, Italy, ...210

Civil Defense, ...30

Class of 1950, ...66

Class of 2000, ...66

Clifftops, Monteagle,
    Tennessee, ...159, 228

Cobb, James, ...56, 62

Coffee High School,
    Florence, Alabama, ...37

Columbia University, ...76

Committee on Environmental
    Design, AIA, ...160

Computers in Architectural
    Practice, ...197

Copenhagen, Denmark, ...83, 205

Cornely, Ed, ...89

Corpus Christi, Texas, ...84

Coventry Cathedral,
    Coventry, ...131, 206

Cravens Hall, Sewanee,
    Tennessee, ...145

Cumberland College,
    Cumberland University,
    Lebanon, Tennessee, ...146, 226

Cypress Land Company, ...35

Davis, Goode, ...132

Deer Lake, ...154

Design/Build, ...216

Design Competitions, ...169

Dickenson County
    Medical Center,
    Clintwood, Kentucky, ...230

The Donelson Fellowship,
    Nashville, Tennessee, ...191, 232

Duncan, Ken, ...215

Durard, Earl, ...48, 171

Dyson, Bert and Ruth, ...43

Eakin Elementary School,
    Nashville, Tennessee, ...173

Ecuador, ...212

Edison Home and Laboratories,
    West Orange, NJ, ...206

Egypt, ... 211

Eisenhower Medals, ... 28

Europe Through The Back Door, ... 209

Evangelism Explosion, ... 39

"Excellence in
   Architecture," 199, 222

Faceted Glass, ... 132

Faith and Form, ... 218

Farmer's Bank and Trust Building,
   Winchester, Tennessee, ... 228

Fez, Morocco, ... xvii

Fifteenth Avenue Baptist Church,
   Nashville, Tennessee, ... 159, 227

First Baptist Church, Athens,
   Alabama, ... 60, 159, 183, 230

Cookeville, Tennessee, ... 193, 234

Cullman, Alabama, ... 158, 227

Dickson, Tennessee, ... 232

Hendersonville, Tennessee, ... 182, 231

   Joelton, Tennessee, ... 199, 233

   Lenoir City, Tennessee, ... 233

   Nashville, Tennessee, ... 131, 225

   Pasadena, Texas, ... 180, 232

   Smyrna, Tennessee, ... 193, 234

White House,
   Tennessee, ... 185, 229

First Christian Church,
   Glasgow, Kentucky, ... 140, 225

First United Methodist Church,
   Athens, Alabama, ... 129, 225

Florence, Alabama, ... 24, 25

Florence, Italy, ... 35

Florence Junior High School,
   Florence, Alabama, ... 35

Florence State College, Florence,
   Alabama, now University
   of North Alabama, ... 65

Forest Hills Baptist Church,
   Nashville, Tennessee, ... 232

Franklin, Aretha, ... 51

Franklin, Jim, FAIA, ... 171

Frank Orr Architects (FOA), ... 153

Galapogos Island, ... 212

Galapogos Islands, Ecuador, ... 212

Garian, Libya, ... 102

Gaudi, ... 210

Genesco, Inc., Nashville,
   Tennessee, ... 168, 228

Gentry, Bob, ... 105

Gentry, Nancy, ... 106

Gettysburg, Pennsylvania, ... 206

Gilbert School,
　Florence, Alabama, ... 35

Gilpin, David, ... 173

Giorgimpopoli,
　Tripoli, Libya, ... 109

The Giza Pyramids, Egypt, ... 212

Goins, Kevin, ... 131

Grand Egyptian Museum, ... 170

The Grand Ole Opry, ... 47

Gresham, Batey, ... 161

Grits, ... 70

Guantanamo Bay, Cuba, ... 84

Guatemala, ... 42

HKS, ... 170

"Hack" Architects, ... 217

Hamilton, Bermuda, ... 205

Hamilton Hall,
　Sewanee, Tennessee, ... 145

Handy, W. C., ... 51

Harpeth Valley Elementary School,
　Nashville, Tennessee, ... 173, 231

Hagia Sofia,
　Istanbul, ... xi, 112, 219

Harrell, Dr. W. A., ... 132

Hart Freeland Roberts, Inc., ... 135

Heery, Inc., ... 173

Henry C. Maxwell Elementary
　School, Nashville,
　Tennessee, ... 175, 233

Hermitage Hills Baptist
　Church, Hermitage,
　Tennessee, ... 186, 230

H. G. Hill Elementary
　School, Nashville,
　Tennessee, ... 146, 226

Hickerson, Clay, ... 161

Hickerson-Fowlkes, ... 170

Hickman Elementary School,
　Nashville, Tennessee, ... 175, 233

Holmes, Oliver Wendell, ... 117

Holland, Ken and Lois, ... 41

Honduras, ... 45

Hope in the Ruins, ... 42

Houk, Ed, ... 42, 46, 166

I-440 Business Center,
　Nashville, Tennessee, ... 232

Ibach, Jack, ... 82

Immanuel Baptist Church, Nashville,
　Tennessee, ... 135, 225, 229

Industrial Design, ... 76

Istanbul, Turkey, ... xi, 112

Jackson, Andrew, ...35

Japan, ...212

Jasper, Alabama, ...24

Joe L. Evins Appalachian Center for Crafts, DeKalb County, Tennessee, ...172, 228

Johnson, Jimmy, ...26, 31

Jones, Rev. Enoch, ...159

Jones, Faye, FAIA, ...145

Jordan, Ralph, "Shug," 78

Judson Baptist Church, Nashville, ...137, 225, 232

Junior Commandos, ...30

Keeble, Edwin A. Associates, Inc., ...(EAK), 128

Kelly Air Force Base, San Antonio, Texas, ...92

Killer Peanut Butter and Jelly Sandwich, ...73

Knodel, Bruce, ...121, 211

Knowles, Ralph, ...120

Korean War GI Bill, ...119

Korean War, ...64

Kreyling, Christine, ...161

Lackland Air Force Base, San Antonio, Texas, ...98

"The Lady of Garian," 102

Lake Providence Missionary Baptist Church, Nashville, Tennessee,ix, ...175, 195, 220, 233

"The Legend of the Lost," 101

Leptis Magna, Libya, ...101

Libya, ...214

Linden Valley Baptist Conference Center, Linden, Tennessee, ...170, 233

Liberia, ...44

Life and Casualty Building, ...142

LifeWay Christian Resources, ...130

Linear and Non-Linear Thinking, ...197

Lintz, Austria, ...21

The Living Bible, ...67

Little Creek, Virginia Marine Base, ...85

Livorno, Italy, ...99

London, ...209

Loren, Sophia, ...101

Lunsar, Sierra Leone, ...43

Lustig, Ron, ...161

Lynch, ...21

Lynch, John Franklin, ...23

Lytle, Andrew, ...146

Machu Picchu, Peru, ...212

Madison, President James, ...35

Madrid, Spain, ...210

Malloy, Bob, ...41

Mark Twain Home,
　Hartford, Connecticut, ...206

Marshall Space Flight Center, ...117

Marty, Edward, ...82, 122

Master Planning, ...159, 180, 181

Maxwell, Rev. Bruce, ... ix, 175

Mazda Miata, ...94

McClinton, Paul and Eugenia, ...61

McCready Hall, Sewanee,
　Tennessee, ...145

McGill, Chris, ...43

McGivney, Jerry, ...118, 183

Merit Music Building, ...179, 229

Metro Nashville
　School Board, ...173

Monteagle Assembly,
　Monteagle, Tennessee, ...145, 226

Monticello, Virginia, ...206

Mont St. Michelle, France, ...208

Moore, Ed and Helen, ...206

Moore, Mary Katherine, ...27

Morocco, ... xvii, 212

Mount Vernon, Virginia, ...206

Museum of Modern Art, ...106

Music City USA, ...41

"Mussolini Modern," 100

Naples, Italy, ...99

NASA, ...117

NASCAR, ...94

Nashville Civic Design Center,
　(NCDC), ...162

Nashville Urban Design
　Forum, ...161

Natchez Trace, ...35

Naval ROTC, ...63, 76, 97, 204

New Hope Baptist Church,
　Hermitage, Tennessee, ...185, 230

Newman, Julian, ...59

New Zealand, ...204

North Boulevard Church
　of Christ, Murfreesboro,
　Tennessee, ...186, 231

Notable Nashville Architecture, 1930 – 1980,.............136, 147, 218

Notre Dame, Paris,........................209

Oaklands Mansion, Murfreesboro, Tennessee,.........176

Ogesby, Bob,...................................161

Old Orchard Shopping Center, Henderson, Kentucky,...............227

Old Salem, Winston Salem, North Carolina, ...206

Orr Family:

    Amy Ruth,..............................48, 52

    Frank Howard, Jr.,.............. xvii, 22

    Franklin Howard,........................22

    Johnny Lynch,...... xviii, 23, 68, 75, 89

    Karen Diann,...............................48

    Lola Ruth Lynch, ... xviii

        Louis (Louie), ...28

        Erin Marie, ...50

    Mark Daniel, ...48, 118

    Nancy Gayle Gentry,............ vii, xi, 68, 111, 105, 115, 166

    Penina Ratliff, ...22

    Robert Allen,.............. xviii, 23, 75

Ryan Lee, ...50

Steven Gentry,..........................49, 118

Orr, Frank Marion,.........................120

Orr, Hubert, ...124

"Orr-Bits,"......................................59

"Orrie,".....................................22, 32

Orr/Houk and Associates, Architects, Inc. (O/H), ...135, 165

Otey Parrish Church, Episcopal, Sewanee, Tennessee,.................150

Overseas Adventure Travel (OAT),..212

Our Savior Church, Copenhagen, Denmark,............205

Panama,...................................45, 177

Parallel Chronologies,.................... xvi

Paris,..207

The Pantheon, Rome,.....................172

Passion, ...215

The Passion of The Christ,..............198

Perry Memorial Hospital, Linden, Tennessee,............177, 229

Peru, ...212

Pisa, Italy,..99

The Plan of Nashville, PoN, ...162

248

Poland, ...45

Pompidou Center, Paris, ...209

Portugal, ...45

Postmodern,
    Postmodernism, ...132, 222

Proverbs 3:4-6, ...66

Pro Bono Work, ...176

Professional Practice in
    Architecture, ...162

Protestant Chapel, Dachau,
    Germany, ...219

Provence, France, ...210

Puns, ...21

Queen Hatshepsut's Temple,
    Egypt, ...122, 211

Quiggle, Mary Lynch, ...23, 81

Race Relations, ...34

Raney, Bobby, ...59, 86

Redstone Arsenal, ...117

Richard Petty Driving
    Experience, ...94

Ridgecrest Baptist Conference
    Center, Ridgecrest,
    North Carolina, ...157, 227

Ridgecrest Baptist Church,
    Madison, Mississippi, ...186, 231

Risher, Chris, ...122

Robbins, Mike, ...131

Rome, ...xi

The Roman Coliseum, Rome, ...113

Ronchamp Chapel, ...140, 209

Rosenbaum House,
    Florence, Alabama, ...27, 34

Rothenburg, Germany, ...205

Rotterdam, Holland, ...84

Rowdy, ...32

Royal Ambassadors, RA's, ...33

Rue Cler, Paris, ...209

Sabratha, Libya, ...101

Sacred Space, ...218

The Sahara, Morocco, ...214

Salisbury Cathedral, England, ...207

The Salvation Army, Madison,
    Tennessee, ...191, 233

Sannoner, Fernand, ...35

Sauerkraut, ...70

Scale in Architecture, ...80

Scanlon, Clark and Sara, ...42

The Scan-it, ...58

School of Architecture
and the Arts, Auburn
University, ...80

School of Architecture,
Auckland University,
Auckland, New Zealand, ...205

School of Architecture,
Victoria University,
Wellington, New Zealand, ...205

Servant Architect, ...223

The Serengeti, Tanzania, ...214

Sewanee Military Academy, (SMA),
Sewanee, Tennessee, ...145

Shadowbluff Apartments,
Nashville, Tennessee, ...229

Sidco Drive Off/ Warehouse
Development, Nashville,
Tennessee, ...229

Shocco Springs, Alabama, ...40

Sibley, Jimmy, ...108

Sierra Leone, West Africa, ...43, 177

Simpson, Amanda, ...32

Smith, Alexander McCall, ...xv

Smith, Don, ...26

Smith, Jerrold, ...195

Smith, L. C., ...80

Smyrna Nursing Home,
Smyrna, Tennessee, ...227

Smyrna, Turkey, ...112

"Sobro", "South of Broadway," 161

Song of Solomon 8:7, ...105

Sorghum, ...72

Souq el Jouma, Libya, ...101

The Southern Baptist
Convention, ...133

The Southern Baptist Sunday
School Board,
(BSSB), Nashville,
Tennessee, ...130, 154, 227

Southern Baptist Theological
Seminary, Louisville,
Kentucky, ...75

Southoaks Office/Warehouse
Distribution Center,
Nashville, Tennessee, ...230

Sparks, Jim, ...xviii

Sparta Church of Christ, Sparta,
Tennessee, ...141, 226

The Sphinx, Egypt, ...211

"Star" Architects, ...217

Ste. Chappelle, Paris, ...209

St. Mont Michelle, France, ...208

St. Paul's Cathedral. London, ...xiii

St. Peter's Basilica and Square,
Rome, ...xiii

Steves, Rick, ... 209

Sunbeam Alpine, ... 94

Stonehenge, ... 207

Sunday School, ... 41

Sustainability, ... 156

Switzerland, ... 209

Tanzania, ... 212

Tate, Allen, ... 146

Tewell, Tommy, ... 26

Tennessee Baptist Adult
    Homes, Inc., ... 154

Tennessee Baptist Children's
    Homes, Inc., Nashville and
    Chattanooga, Tennessee, ... 229

Tennessee Baptist Convention, ... 176

Tennessee River, ... 29

Tennessee Society of Architects, ... 160

Tennessee Valley Authority,
    (TVA), ... 28

Thailand, ... 212

Theta Chi Fraternity, ... 82

Thomasson, Stan, ... 120

Thompson. Regina, ... 131

Trevi Fountain, Rome, ... 113

Tripoli, Libya, ... xi, 92, 98

Tuberculosis Projection Club,
    (TBPC), ... 60, 99

Tuck, Seab, FAIA, ... 161

Two Rivers Baptist Church,
    Nashville, Tennessee, ... 181, 228

Tyler, Jack, ... 149

Union University,
    Jackson, Tennessee, ... 68, 75

The United States Air Force,
    USAF, ... xi, 40, 97

The United states Foreign
    Service, ... 117

University of Alabama, ... 82

The University of the South,
    Sewanee, Tennessee, ... 144, 226

US Army Corps of Engineers, ... 204

USS Albany, ... 83

USS Patch, ... xi, 111

Vanderbilt University,
    Nashville, Tennessee, ... 137

Vanderbilt University
    Medical Center, (VUMC),
    Nashville, Tennessee, ... 177, 230

Vandiver, Libby Lynch, ... 23, 47

Vernazza, Italy, ... 211

Venice, Italy, ... 210

Villa Maria, Tripoli, Libya, ...109

"Visioning," 159

Vitruvius, ... xvii

WSM, Nashville, ...47

W. T. Grant Store,
　　Cookeville, Tennessee, ...226

Waechter, Hank, ...143

War Bonds, ...30

The War Effort, ...30

Warterfield, Charley, FAIA, ...136

Wayne, John, ...101

Wheelus AFB, Tripoli, Libya, ...107

Whitten, Jonathan, ...194

Whitten-Stovall, Bonna, ... xviii

White, Elbridge and Sara, ...136

Whitwell Medical Center,
　　Whitwell, Tennessee, ...229

Whitman, Walt, ...203

Whitt's Barbeque, ...71

Wiley, Boonie Hendricks, ...56

Willetts Studio, Philadelphia, ...132

Williams, Hank, ...51

Williamsburg, Virginia, ...206

Willow Creek Community
　　Church, ...193

Woodmont Baptist Church,
　　Nashville, Tennessee, ...41, 158

Wood, Bobby, "Stink," 64

World War II, ...27

Wright, Frank Lloyd, ...27

Wynette, Tammy, ...51